A Quick Guide

Boxing

The Manly Art of Self-Defense

Published 1923

by
Watanabe Yujiro
Koriyama Kokichi

Translation by Eric Shahan
Foreword by Keith Vargo

Foreword

Foreword

The translator of this book, Eric Shahan, is best known for publishing forgotten classics of Japanese martial arts. In over 40 translations, he has brought antique works on jujutsu, karate, kenpo, swordsmanship and many other indigenous Japanese fighting arts to English-speaking audiences for the first time. This time Eric has done something different. He has translated one of the first books written in Japanese on an imported fighting art: Western boxing.

Of course, there are many excellent boxing manuals in English already. What makes this one special is that it has a unique place in boxing history. "A Quick Guide to Boxing" (or *Kento Jutsu Boxing Haya Wakari* in Japanese) is a valuable record of two things. First, it shows the boxing skills that were taught in Japan's first professional boxing gym, the Japan Boxing Club (Nihon Kento Club) in Tokyo. Second, it indirectly shows the boxing skills and knowledge that were developed in the Black community in the United States at the turn of the 20th century. These were passed on to Japanese boxers via the original author, Yujiro Watanabe, who learned to box from a Black coach in California.

As a record of the skills taught to Japan's first professional boxers, Shahan's translation offers a badly needed corrective. The consensus is that pre-war Japanese boxers were all attack and no defense. But this is likely because promoters and fans wanted to see knockouts and the fighters obliged them by slugging it out. What this book shows is that Watanabe knew both how to hit and how to avoid getting hit, skills must have taught to his fighters. They may have been discouraged from fighting defensively, but they clearly were taught how.

As a record of boxing skills taught by a Black trainer/fighter in early 20th century America, this book may be unique. Boxing manuals from that period were mostly written by white men. However, Yujiro Watanabe was turned away from the white gyms of that era in San Francisco. It was a Black man, Rufus "Rufe" Turner, who welcomed Watanabe into his gym and trained him. Under Turner's tutelage, the founder of Japanese boxing eventually became a champion. Eric helpfully documents Watanabe's rise to the championship level through numerous contemporary newspaper clippings, which are included in this book's appendix. Because a successful fighter makes adjustments and learns more than he's taught, some critics may make the point that the techniques here aren't a carbon copy of what Watanabe learned from his coach. But considering that Watanabe knew nothing about boxing before entering Turner's gym and left it a champion, there is no doubt that much of what you see here is a record of what he learned from Rufe Turner.

In addition to being an important piece of boxing history, this book is also a sound introduction to old-school boxing technique. Although there are some differences from modern boxing noted in the text (e.g. using a backfist is against the rules in boxing now), most of what you see in these pages is still valid. With the help of a qualified boxing trainer, you could take the techniques here and use them in sparring or in a match now. That makes "A Quick Guide to Boxing" a rare find; a book that has both practical and historical value.

Again, this is what Eric Shahan is about. His many translations of old Japanese books on fighting arts have brought valuable knowledge to English-speaking martial artists around the world. Now he has done the same for English-speaking boxing enthusiasts and historians. Enjoy this glimpse into part of boxing's past you never knew.

Keith Vargo
Tokyo, Japan
July 2021

Prologue:
A Brief History
of Boxing in Japan

A Brief History of Boxing in Japan
by Eric Shahan

Sumo versus Boxing and Wrestling

The first boxing matches in Japan were held as part of the ceremonies surrounding the second arrival of the Black Ships commanded by Matthew Perry in 1854.

An illustration showing Commodore Perry and other dignitaries watching Sumo bouts in the 1850s.

To entertain the foreign guests, Koyanagi Tsunekichi 小柳常, along with other Sumo wrestlers, were summoned to Yokohama by the Tokugawa Shogun. First, the wrestlers demonstrated their strength by lifting up bales of rice. Full rice bales weigh about 75 kg/ 165 pounds each. Then they went through their typical training routine.

Koyanagi Tsunekichi 小柳常吉(1817 – 1858)

Later, a bout between Tsunekichi and three sailors from the American ships was arranged. With Commodore Perry and other dignitaries watching the sumo wrestler took on all three sailors at the same time. One he lifted off the ground, the second he locked under his armpit and the third he stomped under his foot. All three were so surprised "their livers were crushed."

Later, in June of Meiji 20 (1887), the first event to feature western wrestlers and boxers was held. It was billed as "Western Sumo." As the poster below shows it also featured Sumo versus boxing and Sumo versus Western Wrestling. In addition over three dozen foreign fighters were featured.

Poster advertising an event with Sumo versus Western wrestlers and fighters 1887

Meriken, Juken and Boxing

Meriken

Before the word "boxing" was used, the word Meriken 米利堅 referred to the pugilist art. It contained the Kanji used for "America" but adds "hard" at the end, so "Hard American-style Fighting." The first boxing, or "Hard American-style Fighting" gym, was established in Yokohama by James Hōjō and Toranosuke Saitō in 1896. It was called the *Meriken Training Institute* メリケン練習所. It was touted as "Fighting with rules." However, the instruction was minimal and the gym soon closed.

Juken

In 1909 Kano Kenji, the nephew of the founder of Judo Kano Jigoro, started the *International Juken "Judo vs Boxing" Club* 国際柔拳倶楽部 in Kobe City. This was an organization that paired Judo practitioners against boxers. Juken "Judo-Boxing" events drew big crowds and were popular into the 1920s, when boxing began to outstrip it.

Advertisement for a Juken Tournament from the 1920s

Boxing

Yujiro Watanabe known as the "Father of Japanese Boxing" and "Four-Round King" retired from boxing in America and returned to Japan in 1921. He founded the Japan Kento "Boxing" Club 日本拳闘倶楽部 in the same year and began teaching what he learned over a decade of boxing in the United States.

An amateur boxing match that took place in Taisho 13 (1924.) The location is a temple inside Ueno Park in Tokyo

WATANABE・KORIYAMA

Boxing:
The Manly Art of Self-Defense

Published 1923

Boxing :
The Manly Art of Self-Defense

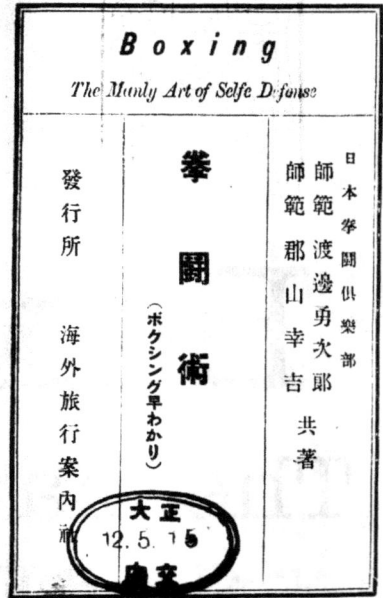

Cover and title page of:

Boxing : The Manly Art of Self Defense
Kento Jutsu
A Quick Guide to Boxing
Japan Kento "Boxing" Club
Authors:
師範　渡辺勇次郎
Shihan (Head Instructor) Watanabe Yujiro
1889 ~ 1956
師範　郡山幸吉
Shihan (Head Instructor) Koriyama Kokichi
1887? ~ ?
Published 1923

The Authors	
Watanabe Yujiro	Koriyama Kokichi

緒言

ボクシング術は百數十年前英國に起り後米國佛國を始め全世界至る處に普及さるゝに至り、殊に歐州大戰以後は其の進歩發展の狀、續く可き者があり、今では、ボクシングを知らざる者は、男子に非ずとまで喧傳さるゝに至つた、然るに日本では、從來之を「メリケン」と稱して、喧嘩の道具にのみ用ゆる鬪牛的の者と誤解してゐた傾きがあつたのは遺憾千萬だが米國に於て十數年間斯術を研究して其蘊奧を極めた渡邊勇次郎氏が數年前日本拳鬪俱樂部を設立し、之に東鄉の名を冠せられて米國に於ける斯界の勇者たる郡山幸吉氏が來り加はつて銳意其の發展に勉められた結果、今では數百名の門人が出來て、旭日東天に昇るが如き勢にて進運に向ひつゝある次第である。

一

Opening Remarks

The art of boxing[1] began several hundred years ago in the United Kingdom. Later, it began to spread to the United States and France, before expanding all over the world. Particularly following the end of the Great European War (World War I) it began spreading and developing at a startling pace. The popularity of boxing has spread so far I can safely say there isn't a boy to be found in the west who doesn't know of boxing. However, it is extremely regrettable[2] that people in Japan seem to be under the impression this is the "American Style" of fighting bareknuckle with no equipment save for their desire to brawl like raging bulls.

However, Watanabe Yujiro spent over a decade training boxing in the United States until he had mastered its inner secrets. He returned to Japan several years ago and founded the Japan Boxing Club. Later Koriyama Kokichi, a man who had made a name for himself in this sport in America, joined the club, crowned with the name "Young Togo" so he was known as Togo Koriyama Kokichi.

He threw himself into the task of training and thanks to his iron will, the club has developed and expanded to several hundred members. This is surely evidence we have achieved a momentum as unstoppable as the sun rising in the east in the morning allowing our organization to thrive.

So then, the ideal method for developing the mind and body begins on the following page. This practical program is, in both theory and science, a complete method for the physical development of the body and mind.

---

[1] The authors use the English word "Boxing" rendered in the Katakana alphabet as ボクシング. The Japanese equivalent is Kento 拳闘, which means "fighting with the fists." For the rest of the book footnotes will indicate when English words are used to describe strikes or techniques.

[2] By "extremely regrettable" the authors use the phrase "this is 1000 X 10,000 degrees of regrettable." At the time boxers wrapped their fists in a leather strap.

さて「ボクシング」は左の點に於て理想的精神修養法なると共に又た實に理論的にも科學的にも完全なる體育養成術だ。

（一）身體の重心を保ちつゝ前後左右に、揮身の力を拳に込めて突き出す者であるから、身體全部適當に活用せられて完全に體育が養成せらる。

（二）自個の身體を安全の地帯に置きながら拳を以つて相手の急所に突撃を加ふるので一度敵の急所を突けば、大象の如き巨漢をも容易に之を倒し得る痛快極りなき護身術だ。

（三）一度競技に望まんか「倒而伺不已」の意氣もて命限り根限り戰ふ譯で觀者をして、血湧き肉躍らしめずんば止まざる者は實にボクシング術だ。然れば、不撓不屈の男性的大勇猛心武士道的精神とを養成せんとするには、ボクシング術を學ぶに若くはない。

1.   It is important to develop your center of balance. You should be able to move forward, back, left or right freely and nimbly. You should be able to leap and turn like a falcon. You should be able to pivot your body and channel that power into your punches. If a fighter is able to use all the parts of his body appropriately this is proof their body is perfectly developed.

2.   While defending every inch of your body, use your fists to strike the enemy in Kyusho, or vital areas. With that impact to the enemy's vital area, you will be able to easily topple even a giant man as big as a full-grown elephant. This is an intensely gratifying self-defense method.

3.   If you ever watch a boxing match, you will see they are filled with the fierce spirit of *Taorete nao Yamazu* (Though I May Fall I Will Not Quit[3]) that pervades the fights. The combatants put their lives on the line as they test the limits of their endurance. The spectators watching can hardly contain themselves as they watch this spectacle which *makes their blood boil and their very flesh dance* (i.e. "is thrilling beyond words.") This is because the art of boxing develops men into tireless and indomitable warriors instills them with a fierce Bushido-like spirit. There is no other way to achieve this other than learning boxing.

---

[3] Kimoto Reiichi wrote about the phrase 倒而尚不已 *Though I May Fall I Will Not Quit* in his history of boxing in Japan called *Modern Fist* 拳の近代.

Watanabe included this phrase which was the slogan of his boxing gym, The Japan Boxing Club, and it emphasizes the importance of maintaining your form.

Kimoto also proposes an origin for this slogan:

The phrase recalls the line from *The Analects by Confucius*, 死而後 已 *Shishite nochi Yamu I Will Stop After I die*. This line was particularly popular with the Soshi, swaggering young men in their prime, in the Meiji Era (1868-1912.) Watanabe was no doubt familiar with it.

此の意味にて、兹に、**ボクシング**術圖解を發刊して七千萬大和民族諸氏が容易に之を理解せられ、之を學ばれる様にと志した譯だ。

大正十一年四月上旬

三

This introduction was written for *A Quick Guide to Boxing* which we are publishing in order to easily give the 70 million Japanese citizen an understanding of boxing. It is our sincere wish that you learn this art.[4]

Written in Early April of the 12th year of Taisho (1923)

---

[4] The sports author Shimoda Tatsuo 下田辰雄 wrote about Watanabe's training style in his 1982 book ボクシング見聞記 *Record of Things Seen and Heard in Boxing:*

Watanabe was not the kind of coach that chewed celery and gave theoretical advice. He personally punched his student boxers in order for them to get the feel of pain, with the hope that the student boxers would learn how to react. Watanabe's goal with hitting was for the body to learn through pain. His teaching methodology was to use this in order to develop the boxers so they would be able to strike back.

● ボクシング競技の規則

土俵は八十六尺より廿四尺までの正四角形のものにして、周圍には三本の繩を張り、闘士の**リング**外に出ずるを防ぎ、競技者は靴を穿き、猿股をつけ、兩手には一定したる**グローブ**を嵌め、腰より上の急所を當るのである。一回を**ラウンド**と稱し、三分間づゝ一分間の休憩を置いて既定の回數まで試合ふものである。若し試合中一方が急所を打たれ例されたる場合は、十秒以内に立ち上つて試合を繼續するに非ざれば**ナツクアウト**と稱して負けとなります。既定の回數に至るも**ナツクアウト**無き時は術の上手の者を勝とし、瓦角の場合は引き分けとなります。昔時は試合の回數等に制限なく一方が**ナツクアウト**されるまで競技した爲め一組の勝負を二日掛りで決定し

Rules for Boxing Competitions

Sumo wrestling uses a raised mound of earth called a Dohyo for matches, however in boxing this is called a "ring." It is a square 16 Shaku by 24 Shaku, 4.8 X 7.3 m/ 15.9 X 23.87 ft. There are three ropes around the edges to prevent the fighters from being knocked out of the ring. The competitors wear leather boots with "monkey thigh" shorts and wear standard gloves on their hands. They use these gloves to strike Kyusho, vital points, above the belt. The bouts are divided into rounds, with each round being 3 minutes with a one minute break in between. The fight goes on for the prescribed number of rounds.

If, during the course of the fight, one of the combatants is struck in a vital area and falls down, if he does not get back up and continue the fight within ten seconds, it is considered a knockout. This means he has lost. If there is no knockout within the allotted number of rounds a decision will be made based on which fighter put on the best display of skill. If both fighters are even the fight is called a draw.

たり、四十二回戦などと云ふ長い回數の競技を成したものですが、

近來は十回以外より最長試合回數を廿回と定められて居ります。競

技の場合、頭突き、肘突き、投、逆及び倒れた相手を攻撃する等の

事は封じられて居ります。

五

Long ago the fights had no limit to the number of rounds, and they continued until one fighter was knocked out. This sometimes resulted in matches that lasted for two days before a winner was declared. There were also bouts that stretched into the 24th round. Recently there are some bouts that go beyond ten rounds, but the limit has been set at 20 rounds. There are some strikes that are illegal, these include: Head-butting, elbow strikes, throws, joint locks and hitting an opponent on the ground. [5]

---

[5] The boxer Sakurada Kojiro 桜田孝次郎 wrote about illegal moves (and provided illustrations) in his 1900 book *Western Boxing: Fully Controlled Offense and Defense* 西洋拳闘術：防撃自在
He writes,
In boxing it is illegal to do throws and so on, if you are in dire straits it may be necessary to rely on them. Therefore you should learn these as well.

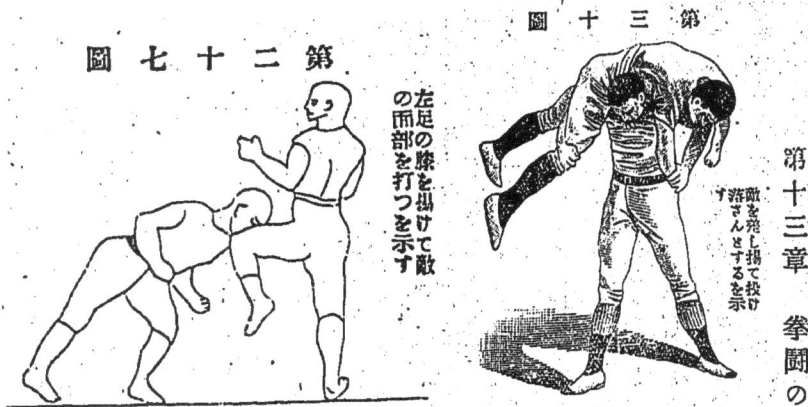

Left: Striking with your left knee into the opponent's face.
Right: Throw the opponent down after you pick him up.

● 公平なる拳闘競技

ボクシング競技は至極公平であります、即ち全世界を共通に左の八種の階級に定め、同階級の闘士同志が試合ふ事が原則となつて居ります。

八種の階級、ウェート級（體量）一〇八斤以下

一バンタム同　一一五斤同
一フェーザァー同　一二二斤同
一ライト同　一三三斤同
一ウエルター同　一四五斤同
一ミッドル同　一五八斤同
一ライドヘビー同　一七五斤同
一ヘビー同　一七五斤以上制限なし

Fairness in Fist Fighting Competitions

Boxing matches are extremely fair. This is explained in the chart below. There are eight designated weight classes and fighters are paired with a person from the same class. This principle is followed all over the world.

The Eight Weight Divisions

Fly Weight   108 Kin[6]   65 kilos   143 pounds
(Handwriting: The words "Paper Weight" are crossed out and "Fly Weight" is written in.)

Bantam Weight	115 Kin	69 Kilos	152 pounds
Feather Weight	122 Kin	73 Kilos	161 pounds
Light Weight	133 Kin	80 Kilos	176 pounds
Welter Weight	145 Kin	87 Kilos	192 pounds
Middle Weight	158 Kin	95 Kilos	209 pounds
Light Heavy Weight	175 Kin	105 Kilos	231 pounds
Heavy Weight	175 Kin and over, no limit.		

---

[6] Kin 斤 is an old unit of weight used in Japan until the late 1940s. 1 Kin is equivalent to 1.3 pounds or 0.6 kilograms.

●日本人世界選手

ボクシングは以上の如く體量によりて階級を定め、各階級に一名づゝで全世界に八名以上の世界選手權者は居らぬのであるが、體量による**競技**なるが故に、體軀小なる日本人と雖も外人に對して何等遜色なく其の階級の名譽ある世界選手權を獲得し得る邦人に最も適當なる運動競技であります。又現今**ライトウエート**級以下の試合が尤も多く歡迎されて居るのであるから此の時に當り國際親善を兼ね廣く日本人を世界に紹介するに絶好の機會であります。殊に日本人は尙武の氣質に富み加ふるに動作の敏捷なる點等に於て日ならずして必ずや此の名譽ある世界選手權を我が日本に屬せしむるは、敢て空想ではありません。此れは去る九月比利賓人パンチ

七

World-Class Japanese Athletes

As was mentioned on the previous page the divisions are divided up by a particular weight range. Further, in each of the eight division there is only one world champion. However, since the competitions are based on weight even Japanese with their smaller stature can compete without any disadvantage against foreign fighters and even attain the honor of World Champion in that division. Thus, I feel this athletic competition is ideally suited to Japanese fighters. Recently there is quite a demand for fighters to compete in Light-Weight division matches and below. Considering the international goodwill that abounds, I think this is an ideal chance to introduce Japanese athletes to the world.

In particular, as Japanese are in possession of a war-like spirit combined with nimble movement, it is clear that the honor of World Champion will inevitably be granted to Japan. This is not just wishful thinking.

ヨービラ氏が米國の ペーパー 級の選手權を掌握した事に依つて證明
が出來ます。

In fact, just this past September, the fighter from the Philippines Mr. Pancho Villa, clinched the Fly Weight division championship. This serves to prove my point.[7]

---

[7] Pancho Villa was the nickname of the boxer Francisco Guilledo (1901 – 1925.)

Francisco was from the Philippines was only 5'1 (154 cm) and weighed around 114 pounds (51 kg). He became the first Asian to win the World Flyweight Championship in 1923. He died suddenly 1925 from complications following a tooth extraction.

Press Photograph of Francisco Guilledo

● 選手ト『チアンピオン』

日本では選手と**チアンピオン**と区別が判然して居らない様ですから、一寸説明を附して置きます。日本で云ふ選手は競技會へ出席するものは皆夫れで、例へば日本拳闘倶樂部選手、關東、關西選手と云ふが如くであるが、歐米の**チアンピオン**なる語は其の階級の一番強いものを云ふので、同じ階級に二人の**チアンピオン**は、存在しないのである。だが地方には地方い**チアンピオン**あり、又各地には其の**チアンピオ**ンなる者が居る。故に一地方い**チアンピオン**が東京の**チアンピオ**

22

Athletes and Champions

In Japan people have trouble distinguishing between the terms "athlete" and "champion," so I would like to take a moment to explain the difference. Most Japanese think of athletes as those who participate in a competitive event. However, for example, the Japan Boxing Club has athletes in the Kanto as well as in the Kansai regions. However, the European Champion or American Champion refers to the strongest fighter in each weight division. There cannot be two champions in the same weight class.

However, each region can have its own Regional Champion and a fighter in each region holds that rank. So then, if the Champion of one region defeats the Champion of Tokyo, that fighter would be the Champion of his home region as well as the Champion of Tokyo.

Along these lines if a Japan Champion were to be carefully selected and defeat the American Champion then the Japanese fighter would hold the Championship of both countries. Further, if he were to topple the World Champion, a Japanese fighter would then become the World Champion.

● 拳闘家ノ報酬

ボクシングは軍隊、學校道場其他有らゆる方面に於て、流行して居るが、一方競技會に於ても各地の都市の常設館にて多きは一週三、四回少くとも一週一回の試合會を催ふし、又年に數回のチアンピオン獲得競技大會が各地に行はれ、其の都度此の人氣や實に驚く可きものにして、入場料の如きも一回の大會に數十萬圓より、數百萬圓

九

A Boxer's Remuneration

At a glance boxing clubs may seem to operate like the popular military or a university martial arts Dojo. However, bouts are organized at facilities in the major cities in each area. Some larger areas have up three or four matches a week and they all have at least one match a week. Further, championship tournaments are held several times a year in all areas, meaning the title is up for grabs. There is always someone popular or something surprising that occurs.

The total admission fees gathered from a single tournament can be from 100,000 yen to the surprising figure of well over 1,000,000 yen (roughly $52,000 ~ $526,000.) This is an amount almost beyond the imagination of Japanese people. Further, the vast majority of this money is divided up between the two fighters. The most powerful fighter in each weight division can amass a world class salary in addition to the achieving the pinnacle of honor.

の多額に上り、到底日本で想像し難い程である。又、其の入場料の大牟は殿打ちの二人間に與へらるゝものなれば、其の階級の如何を問はず有力なる選手は世界最大の報酬を得ると共に、絶大なる名譽を得るものであります。故に選手は攝生を重んじ、酒色を遠ざけて願る、眞面目な生活をして居るものであります。

「附」昨年米國に開催されし米のデムジゐー氏對佛のカルバンチー氏の試合には、入場者九萬餘、入場料十弗より百弗、其の總額三百廿萬圓、勝つた米のデ氏の報酬六十萬圓、負けた力氏が四十萬圓でありました。

Thus athletes go to great pains to take care of their health and avoid both alcohol and the pleasures of the flesh, leading strict lifestyles.

Additional Note

Last year a boxing match held in America last year featuring Jack Dempsey vs Georges Carpeniter was attended by 90,000 people. Ticket prices started at $10 and went up to $100. The total ticket sales exceeded ¥3,200,000 ($1,684,210.) Dempsey received ¥600,000 ($315,000) and the loser received ¥400,000 ($210,000.)[8]

---

[8] A poster advertising the Dempsey vs Carpeniter fight.

日本拳闘倶樂部本部に於ける創設者渡邊東
郎両氏と日本拳闘倶樂部本部前に
日本拳闘倶樂部史上第一回の運手權者萩野、横山両
氏及び日本權手選者萩野、横山両

日本拳闘倶楽部本部前に於けるけ倶楽部,創設者渡邊氏と東郷
郡山師範及び日本歴史事一回の兩選手權者萩野。横山爾氏

Photograph 1
In front of the Japan Kento "Boxing" Club Headquarters.
Pictured are the founder Watanabe and Head Instructor Togo
Koriyama. Also pictured are the historic first Japanese
Champions Okino and Yokoyama.

【第 二 圖】

構　へ

（A）足の「ポジション」左足を相手に向つて直線に出す、右足は六十乃至七十度の角度を以て一尺乃至一尺五寸の間を隔て、後方に踵を擧げて爪先に立ち、常に前後左右に活動し得べき位置に置く。

（B）上体は、對手に斜に向ける事、左手は對手の頤に向け少し曲め、右手は自身の頤の稍々下に力を入れずに、圖の如く構ふ。

（C）顔面は對手に向け頤は稍々引き加減に構へ、眼は常に敵の目を注視す。

Photograph 2
Stances

A. **How to position your feet**. Your left foot should be pointed directly at your opponent with your right foot behind. Your right foot should be between 1 Shaku and 1 Shaku and 5 Sun (30 ~ 45 cm) behind your left foot and angled between 60 ~ 70 degrees. The heel of your back foot should be off the ground so you are standing on the toes of that foot. You should be able to freely move in any direction, forward, back left or right in order to position yourself.

B. **Upper Body.** Your upper body should be angled toward your opponent. Keep your left arm slightly bent as you aim it at your opponent's jaw. Keep your right fist just below your jaw. However, your hand should be relaxed. The Kamae, or stance, is as shown in the photograph.

C. **Face.** Your face should be oriented towards your opponent with your jaw pulled slightly inward. Always keep your eyes focused on your opponent.

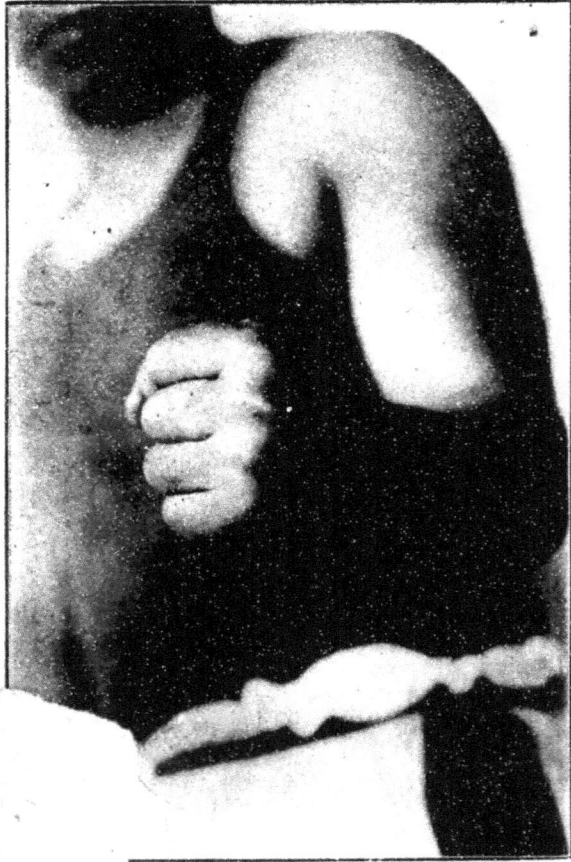

第 三 圖

【第三圖】

手の握り方

手は常に軽く拳を握り對手の急所に當てんとする瞬間に堅く圖の如く握りしめるべし。

Photograph 3.1
How to Make a Fist

Your hand should always be in a loose fist. The moment you strike one of the opponent's Kyusho, vital points, you squeeze your fist tight.

圖に示す拳の個所を以て當る事。

第 三 圖 ノ二

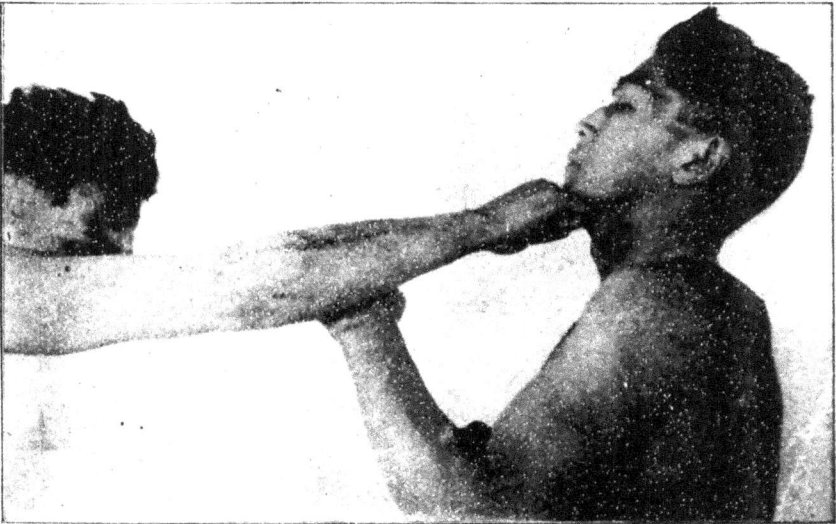

Photograph 3.2
How to Connect with Your Fist

The photograph shows striking with one part of the fist.

【第四圖】

突き出し方（ストレイトライト）

對手の隙を見出すや否や、後に引かず、左右何れの手にて
も、構へたる位置より直ちに揮身の力を込めて、突撃を與
ふる事、但し其の場合にも決して體をくずさざること、多
くの場合には、左手にて突撃を加ふる時は左足に力を集注
す、右手にて突撃を與ふる場合には、左足に重心を置く事
に注意すべし。

Translator's Note: There may have been a printing error on this page since both the instructions say to keep your weight on your left foot for both a left and a right punch. There are even some hand written notations on this page from a previous owner. I have corrected it in the translation.

34

Photograph 4
How to do a Straight Punch[9]

This is a punch you throw the moment you see an opening. Don't pull your fist back first. You can punch with either your left or right hand. From whatever stance you are in, twist your body to generate power in your hips and land your blow. However, be sure to not lose your balance. Generally speaking, when punching with your left hand, you will focus all your power in your right foot. When striking with your right fist be sure to focus on putting your center of balance on your left foot.

---

[9] The title is in Japanese with a handwritten note added by an unknown person. The handwritten note writes the words "Straight Right" phonetically in the Katakana alphabet as ストレイトライト.

【第五圖】

急所

急所を分ちてナックアウト、及びナックダウンの二つ—ナックアウトとは一撃の下に敵を昏睡狀態に陷らしむ。處にして左の四個處とす。

（A）頤　（チギンブロー）　（B）水　月　（ミヅオチ）ソーラープレキサス（パンサ）（スマックブロー）

（C）心　臟（ハートブロー）（D）兩耳の後下部（アンダーゼエアーッブロー）

ナックダウンとは徹底的に敵を倒すナックアウトの如く過激に非ずして一瞬間對手を倒す急所にして左の四個處なり。

（イ）頭部全体　（ロ）顏面及胸部

（ハ）肝臟腎臟　（ニ）腹部全体

第　五　圖

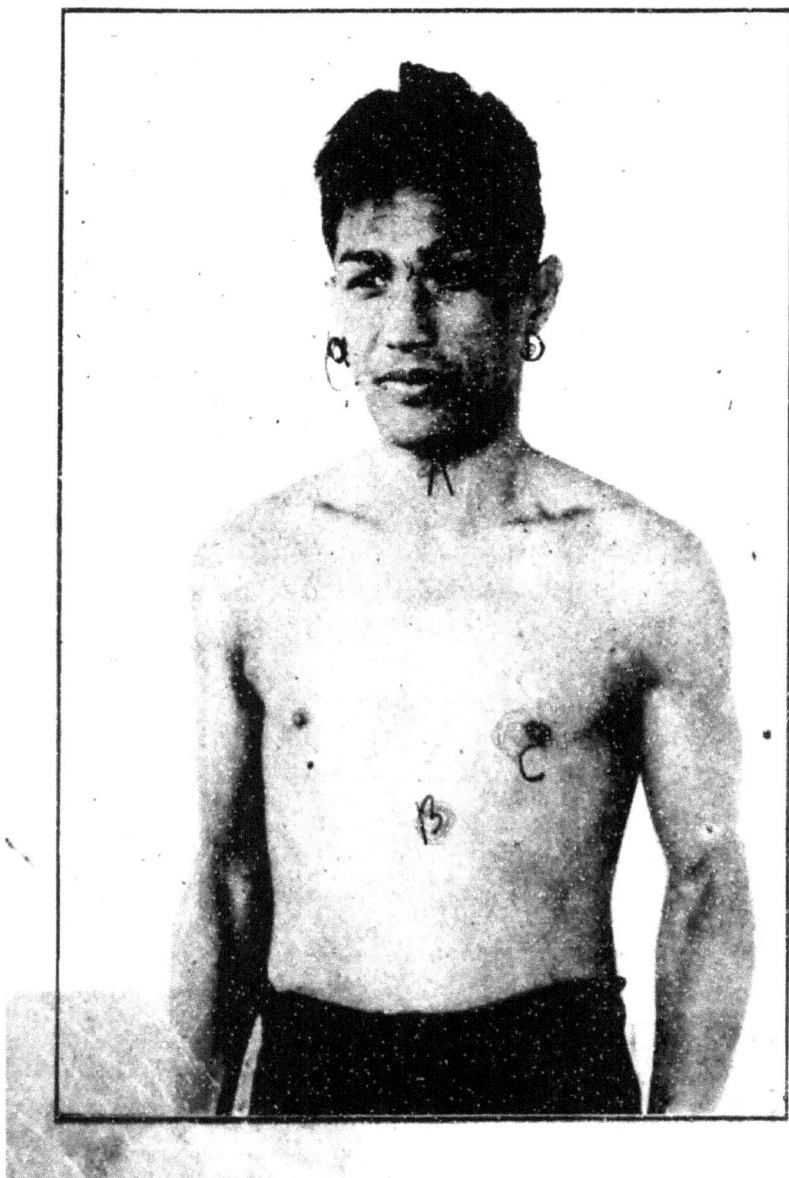

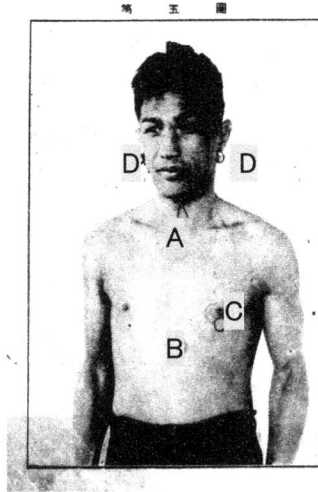

Photograph 5
Kyusho Vital Points

If you are knowledgeable about Kyusho, Vital Points, then you can achieve either a knockout or knockdown. A knockout is when you strike the opponent with a single blow that renders him unconscious. The following four points are ones that can achieve this.

A. Ago Chin (Handwriting : Chin Blow)
B. Suigetsu, also known as Mizu Ochi Solar Plexus (Handwriting: Solar Plexus Punch. Smack Blow)
C. Shinzo Heart (Handwriting: Heart Blow)
D. Ryo Mimi no Ushiro Kabu Spot Just Below and Behind the Ears (Handwriting: Under the Ear Blow.)

A Knockdown is when you completely topple the opponent but the blow was not intense enough to knockout your opponent. The four Kyusho, Vital Points, that will enable you to temporarily topple your opponent are listed below.

1. Tobu Zentai Anywhere on the Head
2. Ganmen Oyobi Kyobu The Face or the Chest
3. Kanzo Jinzo The Liver or the Kidneys
4. Fukubu Zentai The Entire front of the Abdomen

【第 六 圖】

ナックアウト撃の修養

ナックアウトの急所と雖も、打撃軟弱なれば効果を奏せざるが故に、苟も拳闘家たらんとする者、及拳闘術を學ばんとする者は、此の修養の必要なるを忘る可からず。其の方法を示せば先、づ圖の如き砂袋を作りて天井より吊るし、其れを目的に左右兩手を以て逃べたる如く、身体の重心を崩さずして或は近づき或は遠ざかりつ〻、揮身の力を込めて毎日三分位づ〻二三回位之を突撃する練習を成す時には、ナック知らず〳〵の間に身体鐵の如く鍛へらる〻と共に、ナックアウトの名手となるべし。

第　六　圖

Photograph 6
How to Develop your Knockout[10] Punch

Even if you are aware of the previously mentioned Kyusho, Vital Points, if your punch is weak it will not be effective. Thus, if you are dedicated to becoming a Kento-ka, a Boxer, or are training in Kento-Jutsu, the Fist-fighting Art, you should not neglect to develop this important aspect.

As to how to go about this, please refer to the photograph. A Suna-bukuro, Sandbag, is suspended from the ceiling and you will use that as a target as you punch with your left and right hands. When doing this be sure to maintain your center of balance and make sure your distance is neither too close nor too far away. Use the power of your upper body pivoting as you strike. You should punch for 3 minutes two or three times on a daily basis. If you maintain this schedule at some point you will realize your body has become hard as iron and, at the same time, you have developed the knockout punch of a famous boxer.

---

[10] The authors use a combination of the English word "Knockout" rendered as ナックアウト plus the Kanji *Geki* 撃 meaning "Attack or Strike"

【第 七 圖】

距離の判定及び時間の干係

拳闘術に就ては、動作の隼の如く俊敏なるを要すると同時に、距離と時間の干係を判定する事、最も必要なるが故に、圖の如き空氣を中に入れたるボンチングバックと稱する者を吊るし、之を打てば反動によりて電の如く反撥し來るを左右の手を以て巧に之を突けば、其の練習によりて距離と時間との干係を突瑳の間に判定し得る能力を習慣的に修錬する事を得。

Photograph 7
Judging Distance and Its Relation to Timing

When studying Kento-Jutsu, the Art of Boxing, it is essential that you are able to move rapidly and switch directions instantly like the nimble Japanese Tsubasa falcon. At the same time you must also be able to judge distance and understand its relation to timing. Since this is the most fundamentally important skill for a boxer, the training device shown in the photograph has been developed.

This is an air-filled ball called a "punching-bag," which is hung from the ceiling. When struck, it flies back at you like a bolt of lightning. You have to train your left and right hands to deftly strike the "punching-bag." This kind of practice will develop the ability to understand the relation between distance and timing. The ability to make decisions in the barest instant will become habitual.

【第八圖】

稽古開始

以上によりて拳闘術の大略を解し、其豫備智識を修得したる後は、直ちに稽古に取りかゝるを順序とす。先づ靴を穿き猿股を着け、稽古用手袋を兩手にはめ、時間の合圖と共に、雙方より進んでスポートマン的の握手を交はしたる後、打撃の達する距離に身体を置きて、微妙にして機敏なる腦力の働きによりて、休みの合圖ある迄稽古を継續す。其のタイムは三分間にして、休憩は一分間なり。然して、初心者は稽古時間を一回二分間とし、三四回の稽古を最も適當とす。稽古を終る場合には、必ず握手を交はして別るゝ者とす。

Photograph 8
Keiko Kaishi **Beginning Sparring**

This ends the abbreviated explanation of the preparatory exercises for Kento-Jutsu, the Boxing Arts. Having become knowledgeable in these, the next step is going immediately to Keiko, or focused training.

First of all, you will put on boots and Saru-mata, "monkey thigh shorts," and put training gloves on both hands.[11] When the signal is given, both training partners will approach each other and shake hands in a show of good sportsmanship. After that, approach to within striking distance and, using deft movements along with mental judgement, continue with your paired training until the signal to break is given. The time is three minutes per round with a one minute break. However, for beginners, it is best to start with three 2 minute rounds. Always end each training session with a handshake before exiting the ring.

---

[11] Translator's Note: There is no mention of the glove weight in this book however in the 1919 book *The ABC's of Kento (Boxing)*拳闘 の ABC by Sanada Shinchisaburo 眞田七三朗 it says:

Gloves should be new, regulation gloves weighing at least 5 ounces. Gloves for Welter Weight and above should be at least 6 ounces.

【第九圖】 ストレート、レフトを頭に送る

ストレート、レフトとは、即ち左の手を直線に突き出す動作を言ふ者にして、拳闘家に最も大切なる術なり。之れは圖に示す如く、對手が極めて猛烈に突撃し來る場合、もしくは、叩り手を以て來る場合等には、此の術を以つてせば、距離の近きと速力の早さとにて、相手を挫く最も有利の術なり。

Photograph 9
Punching with a Straight Left[12] to Your Opponent's Jaw

A straight left means punching with your left fist in a straight line. This is the most important strike in boxing. This punch is shown in the photograph. It is used to stop your opponent when he launches an intense attack or when he is readying an attack with his dominant hand. If you use this technique at close distance and with speed, it is the most effective way to break an opponent's attack.

---

[12] The authors use the English words rendered in the Katakana alphabet as ストレート、レフト.

【第十圖】

ストレート、レフトを胴に送る

ストレートレフトを胴に送る術は、對手が左右何れかの手にて顔面に突撃し來る場合に、瞬間、上體を圖に示す如く枉げて、右手を以て自身の頤を防ぎながら重心を右足に入れて、左手を以て敵の水月に打ち込む者なり。

第　十　圖

Photograph 10
Punching With a Straight Left to Your Opponent's Abdomen

Use a straight left punch to your opponent's abdomen when he launches a punch to your face with either his left or right fist. In one rapid movement, bend, keeping your right fist guarding your jaw. Placing your weight on your right foot, punch your opponent in Suigetsu, the solar plexus, with your left hand. This is shown in the photograph.

【第十一圖】

ストレート、ライトを頤に送る

此の術は拳闘家が試合の場合非常なる効果を奏し得る者に
して、之を敵に加ふるには、對手が右手を以つて突撃し來
らんとする瞬間、此の術を送る際を見出し、圖に示す如く
右手を以て敵の頤に打込む者なり。

Photograph 11
Punching With a Straight Right[13] to Your Opponent's Jaw

This attack is frequently used by boxers during a bout and it is extremely effective. The way this is applied is to wait until the moment your opponent throws a right punch. Look for when he starts to punch and use that moment to strike him in the jaw. This is shown in the photograph.

---

[13] The authors use the English words rendered in the Katakana alphabet as ストレート、ライト.

【第十二圖】

ストレート、ライトを胴に送る

此の術は圖に示す如く對手が、ストレートライトを以て、我が顔面に打ち來らんとする時、上体を稍〻左方に傾け、左手を以て敵の右手を守りつゝ自身の右手を以て對手の水月に打込む者なり。

Photograph 12
Punching With a Straight Right to Your Opponent's Abdomen

    This technique is done as shown in the photograph. When your opponent is about to throw a right punch to your face, lean your body slightly to the left. Keeping your left hand ready to guard against your opponent's right fist, punch into his Suigetsu, solar plexus, with your right fist.

【第十三圖】

レフト、フックを頤に送る

對手がストレートレフトを以て、顔面に突撃し來らんとする場合、圖に示す如く、己の右手を以て之を左に拂ひ、同時に自身のレフトフックを以て敵の頤に一撃を加ふる者にして、拳鬪術に最も行はれ、然かも有效な突撃法なり。

Photograph 13
Throwing a Left Hook[14] to Your Opponent's Jaw

When you opponent attacks with a straight left punch to your face, respond as shown in the photograph. Use your right fist to sweep his punch to the left and, at the same time, strike him in the jaw with a left hook. This effective technique is one of the most frequently used in boxing because of the intensity of this one blow.

---

[14] The authors use the English words rendered in the Katakana alphabet as レフト、フック. The word "Jaw" is in Kanji 頤.

【第十四圖】

對手のストレート、ライトを自己の
ストレートレフトにて挫く

圖に示す如く、對手が猛烈にして危險なるストレートライトを以て、頤に打ち來る瞬間、我が右手にて相手の左手に充分の注意を拂ひつゝ、上體を少しく前方に進め、直ちに對手の右の内側よりストレート、レフトを敵の頤に送る者なり。此の場合は、左肩を少し高くして、自己の頤を掩へば絕對的に安全なり。

第 十 四 圖

Photograph 14
Breaking an Opponent's Straight Right Punch With Your
Straight Left Punch

As the photograph shows, your opponent has launched a brazen and very dangerous straight right punch. The moment his punch comes for your jaw, lean your upper body slightly forward as you maintain awareness of any possible action from the opponent's left fist, and punch with a straight left along the inside of your opponent's right arm to impact on his jaw. If you raise your left shoulder to conceal your chin, you will be completely protected from his punch.

【第十五圖】

ライト、クロ※スカウンター

圖の如く、對手が、ストレート、レフトを顔面に打込まんとする場合、自己の上体を稍々左方に逃れて、敵の左手は肩を通さしめ、同時に敵の右手を我が左手を以て封じ、自己の右手は九十度内外の角度にて對手の左手の上部を通して頤に命中せしむる者なり。

Photograph 15
Right Cross[15]

As the photograph shows, your opponent has thrown a straight left at your face. Evade this by leaning your body slightly to the left, so that your opponent's left fist passes over your shoulder. At the same time use your left hand to suppress his right fist as you punch with your right fist. If you swing your right fist at about a 90 degree angle it should pass over the top of the opponent's left arm and connect directly with his jaw.

---

[15] The authors use the English words rendered in the Katakana alphabet as ライト、クロス. There is a handwritten note that adds the word "counter", written as カウンター.

【第十六圖】

右スイングを左にて受け、右のアツ
パーカットを頤に送る、

此の術は對手が、右スィングを以て、自巳の頤に打込まん
とする場合、直ちに左手を圖に示す如く側面に擧げて之を
防ぎ、同時に右のアッパーカットを對手の頤に突き上げ、
氣分にて打込む者なり。

Photograph 16
Blocking the Opponent's Right Swing With Your Left Then
Punching With a Right Uppercut[16] to His Jaw

In this situation your opponent has swung at you with his right fist, aiming for your jaw. You immediately respond as shown in the photograph. Raise your left arm to the side, as shown, in order to block his right punch. At the same time, punch your opponent in the jaw with a right uppercut with the feeling of driving in and upward.

---

[16] The authors use the English word "uppercut" rendered in the Katakana alphabet as アッパーカット.

【第十七圖】

左スヰングを右にて防ぎ、左手を水
月に送る

之れは、第十六圖と反對に、左手のスキングを我が頤に打
込み來らんとする場合、右手を側面に舉げて之を止め、同
時に左手を百三十度位の角度に曲げて、對手の水月に打込
む者なり。

Photograph 17
Using Your Right Arm to Block a Left Swing,[17]
Then Punching to His Suigetsu With Your Left

This technique is basically the opposite of what was shown in photograph 16 on the previous page. The opponent swings with his left towards your jaw. Raise your right arm to the side to stop this and, at the same time, bend your arm to about a 30 degree angle and punch into his Suigetsu, solar plexus.

---

[17] The authors use a combination of the Kanji for "left" 左 with the English word "swing" in the Katakana alphabets 左スヰング

【第十八圖】

ダッキング、ライト、スヰングの場合

對手が右スヰングを打ち來る場合、直ちに我が上体を前方にかゞめて、敵のスヰングをして上空を通過せしめ、自己の左右兩手何れかを對手の隙に打込む姿勢なり。

（ダッキングとは、對手の打撃をくゞる術を言ふ）

Photograph 18
Ducking a Right Swing[18]

When the opponent comes at you with a right swing, immediately bend your upper body down and forward, allowing his punch to pass through the air over you. From this position you are able to attack with either your left or right hand, depending on where the opponent is open. The English word "ducking" means to pass under an opponent's punch.

---

[18] The authors use the English words rendered in the Katakana alphabet as ダッキング、ライト、スヰング.

【第十九圖】

サイド、ステップ

圖に示す如く對手が、ストレート、レフトを我が顔面に打ち來る場合、右手を以て左方に拂ひ我が左手を以て上體を守りつゝ、右の側面に向つて、橫飛びに避けて、敵をして長蛇を逸せしむる術なり。

Photograph 19
Sidestep[19]

As the photograph shows your opponent has targeted your face with a straight left punch. Use your right hand to sweep this to your left while using your left hand to guard your body. Twist your right side forward as you spring to the side, escaping.

From the opponent's perspective when you use this technique it is 長蛇を逸す *Choda wo Issu* as if he has allowed a great snake to escape (i.e. "as if a great prize has slipped through his fingers.")

---

[19] The authors use the English word "sidestep" rendered in the Katakana alphabet as サイド、ステップ.

【第二十圖】 ストレートレフト、をストレートライにて挫く

對手がストレート、レフトにて顔面に打ち込み來る場合、左手を以て、對手の右を制止し、自己の右手を對手の左手の内側より頤に打込む者なり。

第 二 十 圖

Photograph 20
Blocking the Opponent's Straight Left with a Straight Right

Use this technique when your opponent punches with a straight left, aiming at your face. Use your left hand to suppress his right fist as you punch him in the jaw with your right fist by angling it along the inside of his left arm.

【第二十一圖】

相手のレフト、スヰングを逃れ、左米7

ツクを頭に送る

對手が左スウィングを我が水月に向けて、打ち込む場合、胴体を稍〻後方にかゞめて、對手をして空を打たしめ、同時に我がレフト、フックを敵の頭に打ち込む者なり。

Photograph 21
Avoid the Opponent's Left Swing and Strike With a Left Hook[20] to His Jaw

In this situation your opponent swings with a left to your Suigetsu, solar plexus. Bend your back slightly backwards, so he only strikes the air. At the same time punch your opponent in the jaw with a left hook.

---

[20] The authors use a combination of the Kanji for "left" 左 with the English word "hook" in the Katakana alphabets 左フック.

【第二十二圖】

フワイター。の姿勢

拳闘家を分ちて二つとす、ボクサー及びフワイター之れなり、前者は重に其の技術を以て離れ術を天才的に發揮するを言ひ、後者は寧ろ其の勢力及びフワイター術を以て、攻勢に出で敵をして其術を施す術なからしむる者を言ふ、されば、フワイターは、常に對手に接近し、或はクリンチしてイン、フワイチングを發揮する者なり。

Photograph 22
Fighter's Stance[21]

There are two different kinds of pugilists: boxers and fighters. The former relies on technical skill to deftly maintain distance until it is time to strike while the latter uses power and aggressive fighting technique against an enemy. However, a fighter will always seek to close the distance with his opponent. Once in close, he will employ clinching and other infighter techniques.

---

[21] The authors use a combination of the English word "Fighter" rendered in the Katakana alphabet as フワイター with the Kanji 姿勢 meaning "Stance."

【第二十三圖】

クリンチ

クリンチとは、稽古もしくは競技中兩者接近して、組合ひたる場合を言ひ、常に兩手共相手の兩手の内側に入るれば、術を施し、又たは術を防ぐ機會甚だ多ければ、組合ひたる場合には、常に我が兩手を相手の内側に入るゝ事を忘る可からす。

Photograph 23
Clinch[22]

A clinch is when two opponents come together during a bout or during training until they are in Kumi Uchi, or intertwined. The way a clinch is normally done is to force both your hands between the hands of your opponent. This is frequently used to prevent your opponent from launching an attack. Be sure to not forget that both your hands should be on the inside of your opponent's hands.

---

[22] The authors use the English word "Clinch" rendered in the Katakana alphabet as クリンチ.

【第二十四圖】

クリンチの塲合、右アッパーカット
を頤に送る

前述の如く、兩手を對手の内側に置き少しく對手を後方に押すと同時に、一步、退きながら、右アッパーカットを頤に打ち込む。

Photograph 24
Striking with a Right Uppercut to the Opponent's Jaw During a Clinch

As was mentioned on the previous page, you have both your hands on the inside of your opponent's hands. If you push him slightly backwards and, at the same time, step back one pace you can strike with a right uppercut to his jaw.

【第二十五圖】

クリンチの場合左スウイングを頭に送る

■に示す如く對手を左右兩手にて重に腹部を攻撃し、敵をして腹部にのみ注意を拂はしめ、其虚に乗じて、左スウイングを敵の右頭に送る。

第 二 十 五 圖

Photograph 25
How to Use a Left Swing to Punch Your Opponent In the Jaw From a Clinch

As the photograph shows, you have used your left and right hands to pummel the opponent's abdomen, causing him to focus his attention there. Using that distraction, swing your left to connect with the right side of his jaw.

【第二十六圖】

右スウイングを左ケデネーに送る

對手が顔面に左手を以て攻撃する場合、自ら對手のケデネーに隙生じ易ければ、此の場合少しく上体を左方に曲げ、對手の右を防ぎつゝ、右スウイングを猛烈に敵のケデネーに打ち込む術なり。

Photograph 26
Using a Right Swing to Strike a Left Kidney Blow[23]

Use this technique when your opponent throws a left punch at your face. This type of punch can easily leave your opponent's kidney wide open. To apply this technique, while guarding against your opponent's right, bend your upper body slightly to the left. Finish the technique by swinging a blow full of fury into his left kidney.

---

[23] The authors use a combination of the Kanji for "Left" 左 with the English word "Kidney" rendered in the Katakana alphabet as 左キデネー.

【第二十七圖】

スウイングをくゞり、右ストレートを心臓に送る

對手が左スウィングを頤に打込み來る場合、上体を稍〻左方にかゝめ、對手の右手に充分の注意を拂ひ、右ストレートを敵の心臓に送る。

第 七 十 二 圖

Photograph 27
Ducking Under the Opponent's Swing and Punching With a
Straight Right to Your Opponent's Heart

Use this technique when your opponent swings at your jaw with his left fist. Respond by leaning your upper body slightly to the left of the centerline. Punch straight into his heart with your right fist, while being careful to guard against your opponent's right fist.

【第二十八圖】

ショートライト、スウィングをくゞ
り左手を對手の胴に送る

此の術は對手が突瑳的にショート、ライト、スウィングを
頭に打込み來る場合、身を前方に沈め、對手の左手を右手
にて封じ、直ちに左手を對手の水月に打込む者なり。

第 二 十 八 圖

Photograph 28
Ducking Under a Short Right Swing[24] and Punching to the Body With Your Left

In this situation, your opponent is punching at your jaw with short, right swings. Respond by sinking your body down and forward and use your right hand to defend against your opponent's left fist. Then immediately punch to your opponent's Suigetsu, or solar plexus, with your left fist.

------

[24] The authors use the English words "Short Right Swing" written in the Katakana alphabet as ショートライト、すウイング. However, it looks like the man on the left is throwing a right cross.

【第二十九圖】

コークスクルー

圖に示す如く、對手が聊か右頤に隙ありて、突擊した合、左手を少しく上方より打下ろし氣分にて、對手の頤に打擊を與ふる者なり。但し、命中せんとする瞬間、拳を內側にひねる。所謂錐もみ術なり。

Photograph 29
Corkscrew[25]

As the photograph shows, use this technique when there is a slight opening near your opponent's jaw on the right side. When he punches, throw a left that starts slightly high and descends to contact his jaw. To achieve a corkscrew blow, you twist your fist to the inside the moment you make contact. In Japanese this is called Kirimomi Jutsu, corkscrew technique.

---

[25] The authors use the English word "Corkscrew" rendered in the Katakana alphabet as コークスクルー.

【第三十圖】

バックハンド、ブロー

己れの發射せる打撃が命中せざる場合或は故意に外づして其の反動を利用し、外拳にて對手の顏、或は顏面に當てる術なり、拳の正面を以てせず、其の外部を利用するが故、バックハンドブローと云ふ

現在ニテハ バツク ハンド ブローは 禁じられて居る。1933.

Photograph 30
Backhand Blow[26]

This technique is used when your initial punch fails to meet its target or is blocked by your opponent. In that case, this technique uses the returning motion to strike your opponent in the jaw or side of the face. Since this strike uses the back of the hand instead of the front, it is called the backhand blow.

A Quick Guide to Boxing
End

---

[26] The authors use the English words "Backhand Blow" rendered in the Katakana alphabet as バックハンド、ブロー. There is a handwritten notation on the left side that says, *The backhand blow has been declared illegal. 1933*

Appendix

Appendix

This next section will reproduce newspaper articles regarding the authors as well as the men that trained Watanabe Yujiro. The boxing records are from Boxrec.com, however the statistics only list the confirmed matches and are just for reference.

The newspapers they are excerpted from are more than a hundred years old and, in some cases, refer to racial and ethnic minorities in a manner that would not be appropriate today. Though this may distress some readers, the decision was made to leave them as is in order to give an accurate historical context. The hope is that this will help readers understand the daily struggles people of color, especially fighters of color, faced in the United States at that time.

The Authors and Their Trainers

Yujiro Watanabe	Koriyama Kokichi

YUJIRO WATANABE, Japanese	YOUNG TOGO, "THE LITTLE DEMON."
Rufus Turner	**Charley Turner**

RUFE TURNER.	

Watanabe Yujiro
25 Bouts 12 Wins (5 KO) 10 Loss 2 Draw
Source: Boxrec

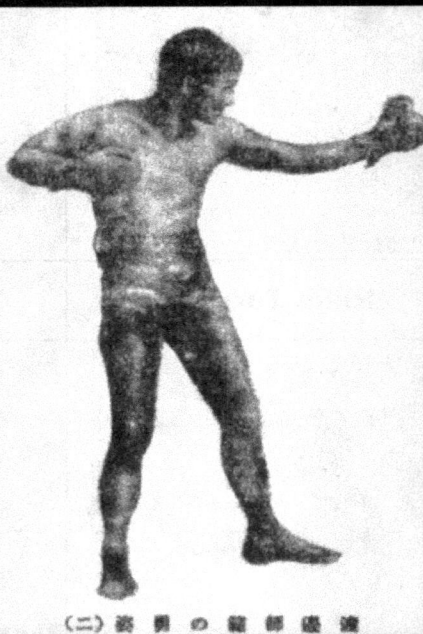

（二）姿男の範師優渡

Watanabe Yujiro: Author

Watanabe Yujiro (1889 ~ 1956) went to San Francisco in 1906 in order to study English and commerce. While living there he got knocked down in a fight with a local which spurred him to begin training in boxing. He described this in an interview for the March 1922 issue of the sports magazine *Baseball World*:

I ran away from my home to America. It was November 3rd of Meiji 39 and I was walking around looking at the carnage that the San Francisco great earthquake had wrought. An American boy spoiling for a fight came up to me and nailed me in the face with a straight punch. That was all it took to lay me out. Up to that point my only goal had been to be a linguist, however my whole focus shifted to becoming a boxer. I wanted to beat the guys that messed with me to a pulp. I found a fighter Rufe Turner, who was a black man, willing to train me and I joined his gym. Later I fought sixteen bouts in a row and won all sixteen. The English language papers in San Francisco described me as "The Top Japanese Fighter in the World Has Emerged!" Around that time I got word from back home that there were boxers eager to learn so in the spring of Taisho 10 after more than a decade away I returned home.

Watanabe was refused admittance to white owned gyms, however he eventually was able to join a gym run by a man named Rufe Turner, a black boxer born in Stockton California. Watanabe trained diligently under Rufus and his brother Charley and had his debut fight in 1908 in California. He won his first bout in a four round decision. In the following year and a half he fought 16 bouts and was undefeated. He got the nickname "King of the Four Rounds" which was in reference to the fact that in California at the time fights were limited to four rounds.

Watanabe's First Bout and Rise to Champion

Watanabe's record on boxing databases is 33 Bouts:
18 Wins with 8 knockouts
11 Losses, 2 Draws
1 Forfeit, 1 Unknown

March 23, 1911
The Oakland Tribune

The fun for the evening was supplied when the matchmaker brought forth C. Marquida and Yu Jivo Watanada (sic) to appear in a four-round contest, the former a Filipino and the latter a Japanese. Marquida is from the Rufe Turner Boxing School of all Nations, and he displayed plenty of aggressiveness, if not knowledge of the game. The Jap was a poor example of the manly art, and if the Japanese army and navy is not made up of braver men than the sample of last night, none of the white nations need fear them..

Bout Caused Much Laughter

Withal the affair was a joke; everybody had a good laugh, and the proof that the rice eaters are not great fighters was amply proven. In the fourth round the Filipino boy was waltzing about the ring in something after the style of his native dance when he let one the hands fly wildly around him and Mr. Jap bumped into it. That was enough; the little brown man who had started so confidently had been shown the error of his ways and he decided that the better part of valor was discretion, so he laid flat on his back until counted out.

October 31ˢᵗ 1911
Oakland Tribune

JAP FIGHTER IS A WONDER.

Al Rogers and Billy Weeks will also
keep things moving, judging by their
sensational mill at the West Oakland
club last week. Their slugging match
was one of the greatest ever seen here
and had the fans rooting like mad men
from the first round until the last. It
was a gory battle and as they are to
fight winner take all tonight, there will
be no stalling or monkey business. It
will be a real scrap and will be worth
watching.

Yujiro Watanabe and Joe Livermore
will furnish the preliminary while a four
round curtain raiser will open the show
at 8:30 o'clock sharp.

Harry Foley will referee all of the contests and matchmaker Moffitt states that
the usual care will be taken to seat
all of his patrons in their proper places.
The advance sale of tickets is now on
at the Mecca.

Jap Fighter is a Wonder

Al Rogers and Billy Weeks will also keep things moving, judging by their sensational mill at the West Oakland club last week. Their slugging match was one of the greatest ever seen here and the fans rooting like mad men from the first round until the last. It was a glory battle and as they are to fight winner take all tonight, there will be no stalling or monkey business. It will be a real scrap and will be worth watching.

Yujiro Watanabe and Joe Livermore will furnish the preliminary while a four round curtain raiser will open the show at 8:30 o'clock sharp.

Harry Foley will referee all of the contests and matchmaker Moffitt states that the usual care will be taken to seat all of his patrons in their proper places. The advance sale of tickets is now on at the Mecca.

May 19th 1911
Oakland Tribune

In the special event Yujiro Watanabe, the Japanese boxer who has been creating a sensation about the bay, will be pitted against Young Turner, and in the first bout of six rounds Henry Hickey will meet Eddie Gibbs. Besides these three six-round contests there will be three four-round preliminaries.

In the special event Yujiro Watanabe, the Japanese boxer who has been creating a sensation about the bay, will be pitted against Young Turner and in the first bout of six rounds Henry Hickey will meet Eddie Gibbs. Besides these three six-round contests there will be three four-round preliminaries.

August 22nd 1911 Oakland Tribune

FOUR ROUNDERS TO SHOW.

SAN FRANCISCO, Aug. 22. — The four rounders will hold the boards next Friday night, when Manager Louis Parente of the White Rock club will stage his all star card. It is one of the best short distance boxing cards that has been offered the fans in some time, and some exciting milling should result during the evening.

The showing of Danny O'Brien, the crack northwest lightweight, who is matched with Rufe Turner, will be watched with interest. O'Brien has performed here a few times and has showed himself to be a comer. He meets a seasoned performer in Turner, who knows the game.

Yujiro Watanabe, the Japanese champion, will meet a tough customer in Kid Wayne. The latter is an aggressive chap who likes to mix it, and he will be after the Jap all the time. Watanabe has not yet been beaten, though he has had many fights around these parts.

Four Rounders to Show

San Francisco, Aug.22.- The four rounders will hold the boards next Friday night, when Manager Louis Parents of the White rock club will stage his all-star card. It is one of the best short distance boxing cards that has been offered the fans in some time, and some exciting milling should result during the evening.

The showing of Danny O'Brien, the crack northwest lightweight, who is matched with Rufe Turner, will be watched with interest. O'Brien has performed here a few times and has showed himself to be a comer. He meets a seasoned performer in Turner, who knows the game.

Yujiro Watanabe, the Japanese champion, will meet a tough customer in Kid Wayne. The latter is an aggressive chap who likes to mix it, and he will be after the Jap all the time. Watanabe has not yet been beaten, though he has had many fights around these parts.

November 3rd 1913
Oakland Tribune

Lee Johnson, the local colored lightweight, will meet Babe Picato, the globe trotter, in one of the special events, and Kid Exposito and Togo Watanabe will also get together. Dick Kendall vs. Dummy Thomas, and Joe Reilly vs. Kid Romeo are other attractive bouts on the card.

* * *

Lee Johnson, the local colored lightweight, will meet Babe Picato, the globe trotter, in one of the special events, and Kid Exposito and Togo Watanabe will also get together. Dick Kendall vs. Dummy Thomas, and Joe Reilly vs. Kid Romero are other attractive bouts on the card.

September 1th 1914 Oakland Tribune

FOUR ROUND PROGRAM A POOR JOKE

As usual, the four-round bouts across the bay left an unpleasant taste in the mouths of the unfortunate spectators. Charlie Miller, the heavyweight joke, lay down to Harry Wills, the negro, after one minute of burlesque fighting. Otto Berg was declared the winner over Al Rodgers on a foul in the first round. Jack Morris and Jack Kelly, two big dub substitutes, staggered through four rounds to a draw. The police stopped the Soldier Woods-Mugsy McGraw bout. Tommy Stevens won in four rounds over Joe Getz. Joe Thomas, colored, was knocked out in one round by Battling Brant. Young Watanabe knocked out Joe Carroll in the second round. Young Hyland knocked out Dick Keller in the first round.

The matches were so unevenly made that the crowd got nothing for its money, the show being over by 10 o'clock.

Four Round Program a Poor Joke

As usual, the four-round bouts across the bay left an unpleasant taste in the mouths of the unfortunate spectators. Charlie Miller, the heavyweight joke, lay down to Harry Wills, the negro, after one minute of burlesque fighting. Otto Berg was declared the winner over Al Rodgers on a foul in the first round. Jack Morris and Jack Kelly, two big dub substitutes, staggered through four rounds to a draw. The police stopped the Soldier Woods-Mugsy McGraw bout. Tommy Stevens won in four rounds over Joe Getz. Joe Thomas, colored, was knocked out in one round by Battling Brant. Young Watanabe knocked out Joe Carroll in the second round. Young Hyland knocked out Dick Keller in the first round.

The matches were so unevenly made that the crowd got nothing for its money, the show being over by 10 o'clock.

August 9ᵗʰ 1911 The St. Louis Star and Times

JABS AND JOLTS.

BY MAL DOYLE.

Yujiro Watanabe, son of Nippon, the only Japanese boxer in the world, wants to come to St. Louis to "box fight" any man at 130 pounds. In his letter, dated San Francisco, he says in part:

"A cat wild I am. Wolgast some day I box in the nose. I no quit. I'm a game. A hit on the nose it hurts me not. I'm a game."

Get busy you matchmakers. This Jap don't say what kind of a game he is, but I suppose the cross is half tar-boiler and half Jap. Never whipped until dead and the heels cut off.

*   *   *

Jabs and Jolts **By Mal Doyle**

Yujiro Watanabe, son of Nippon, the only Japanese boxer in the world, wants to come to St. Louis to "box fight" any man at 130 pounds. In his letter, dated San Francisco, he says in part:

"A cat wild I am. Wolgast someday I box in the nose. I no quit. I'm a game. A hit on the nose it hurts me not. I'm a game."

Get busy you matchmakers. This Jap don't say what kind of a game he is, but I suppose the cross is half tar-boiler and half Jap. Never whipped until dead and the heels cut off.

Watanabe is probably referring to Adolphus Wolgast (1888 ~1955), who was nicknamed the Michigan Wildcat. Wolgast was the world lightweight champion from 1910-1912. The picture of Wolgast is from that period.

August 22nd 1911 The San Francisco Call

Four Rounders Promise Exciting Sport

The four rounders will hold the boards next Friday night, when Manager Louis Parente of the White Rock club will stage his all star card. It is one of the best short distance boxing cards 'that has been offered the fans in some time, and some exciting milling should result during the evening.

The showing of Danny O'Brien, the crack northwest lightweight, who is matched with Rufe Turner, will be watched with interest. O'Brien has performed here a few times and has showed himself to be a comer. He meets a seasoned performer in Turner, who knows the game.

Yujiro Watanabe, the Japanese champion, will meet a tough customer in Kid Wayne. The latter is an aggressive chap who likes to mix it, and he will be after the Jap all the time. Watanabe has not yet been beaten.

Four Rounders Promise Exciting Sport

The next four rounders will hold the boards next Friday night, when Manager Louis Parente of the White Rock club will stage his all-star card. It is one of the best short distance boxing cards that has been offered the fans in some time, and some exciting milling should result during the evening.

The showing of Danny O'Brien, the crack northwest lightweight, who is matched with Rufe Turner, will be watched with interest. O'Brien has performed here a few times and had showed himself to be a comer. He meets a seasoned performer in Turner who knows the game.

Yujiro Watanabe, the Japanese champion, will meet a tough customer in Kid Wayne. The latter is an aggressive chap who likes to mix it, and he will be after the Jap all the time. Watanabe has not yet been beaten.

August 24th 1911 The San Francisco Call

· FOUR ROUNDERS TO SHINE.

SAN FRANCISCO. Aug. 24. — Danny O'Brien of Portland will have a grand chance to blossom out as a lightweight star tomorrow evening. If this newcomer is successful in his mix-up with Rufe Turner, the old time colored lightweight, he will be boosted right to the front, and the chances are that we will shortly be paying fancy prices to see him perform in the 20 round game.

O'Brien came here an unknown a couple of months ago. He made good at the jump off and it was against Turner that he performed this stunt, too. Danny fought the hurricane negro off his feet about six weeks ago and furnished a sensation by getting a draw with the negro, who had been beating all comers up to that time.

O'Brien is a good two handed fighter and he has a punch in either hand. He is also clever and has a good head. He knows what to do in a pinch, which is more than a whole lot of them with twice his experience know. He always trains hard for a fight, and it looks as though he will be in the pink of condition when he goes against Turner tomorrow evening.

The old negro will rely upon his skill and his experience to beat the youngster. He knows that he lacks the old time dash and the wonderful punch which he used to have in stock, but he still retains that great skill with the mitts. He can still block with any of them and he has forgotten more good tricks than most of the youngsters ever have learned.

Young Watanabe, the only Japanese who ever made a success of the boxing game, is on the job and ready for his mill with Kid Wayne, a promising young local lightweight. The Jap is without doubt one of the cleverest of the four round boys in his class and if he beats Wayne decisively he will be in line for a main event the next time he starts.

Four Rounders to Shine

San Francisco, Aug. 24. – Danny O'brien of Portland will have a grand chance to blossom out as a lightweight star tomorrow evening. If this newcomer is successful in his mix-up with Rufe Turner, the old time colored lightweight, he will be boosted right to the front, and the chances are that we will shortly be paying fancy prices to see him perform in the 20 round game.

O'Brien came here an unknown a couple of months ago. He made good at the jump off and it was against Turner that he performed this stunt too. Danny fought the hurricane negro off his feet about six weeks ago and furnished a sensation by getting a draw with the negro, who had been beating all comers up to that time.

O'Brien is a good two handed fighter and he has a punch in either hand. He is also clever and has a good head. He knows what to do in a pinch, which is more than a whole lot of them with twice his experience know. He always trains hard for a fight, and it looks as though he will be in the pink[27] of condition when he goes against Turner tomorrow evening.

The old negro will rely upon his skill and his experience to beat the youngster. He knows that he lacks the old time dash and the wonderful punch which he used to have in stock, but he still retains that great skill with the mitts. He can still block with any of them and he has forgotten more good tricks than most of the youngsters ever have learned.

Young Watanabe, the only Japanese who ever made a success of the boxing game, is on the job and ready for his mill with Kid Wayne, a promising young local lightweight. The Jap is without doubt one of the cleverest of the four round boys in his class and if he beats Wayne decisively he will be in line for a main event the next time he starts.

---

[27] "In the pink" means "in very good health."

October 18th 1911

GOLDEN GATE CLUB HAS GOOD CARD FOR FRIDAY NIGHT

The Golden Gate Club offers an attractive card for Friday night at Dreamland pavilion. In the windup Charlie Reilly, the clever local lightweight who has been doing so much training at Al White's camp, will clash with "Kid" Dalton, the tough little scrapper from Los Angeles. Dalton is a two-handed fighter with a punch and as he is always boring in, he should make a good opponent for a scientific lad such as Reilly. This will be the main event of an eight-bout program.

Charlie Miller and Ed Dunkhorst, heavyweights, will tangle in the joke scrap of the night. These two burlies make the scales quiver around the 600-pound mark and there should be lots of fun dispensed when they begin to move about on the platform.

The middleweight go between Kid George and Rufe Williams should be a hummer. These middleweights are well matched and as George has been doing some sensational milling lately he figures to turn the tables on the colored pugilist.

The rest of the card is as follows: Rufe Turner vs. Billy Walters, Dummy Thomas vs. Kid Harvey, Lee Johnson vs. Billy Chappelle; Yujiro Watanabe vs. Kid Schiff and another four-round preliminary.

Golden Gate Club Has Good Card For Friday Night

The Golden Gate Club offers an attractive card for Friday night at Dreamland pavilion. In the windup Charlie Reilly, the clever local lightweight who has been doing so much training at Al White's camp, will clash with "Kid" Dalton, the tough little scrapper from Los Angeles. Dalton is a two-handed fighter with a punch and has he is always boring in, he should make a good opponent for a scientific lad such as Reilly. This will be the main event of an eight-bout program.

Charlie Miller and Ed Dunkhorst heavyweights, will tangle in the joke scrap of the night. These two burlies make the scales quiver around the 600-pound mark and there should be lots of fun dispensed when they begin to move about on the platform.

The middleweight go between Kid George and Rufe Williams should be a hummer. These middleweights are well matched and as George has been doing some sensational milling lately he figures to turn the tables on the colored pugilist.

The rest of the card is as follows: Rufe Turner vs. Billy Walters, Dummy Thomas vs. Kid Harvey, Lee Johnson vs. Billy Chappelle: Yujiro Watanabe vs. Kid Schiff and another four-round preliminary.

May 27ᵗʰ 1912
The Honolulu Advertiser

TODAY DETERMINES IF YAMOGATA WILL BOX SATURDAY

Great interest was created among the local Japanese by the announcement in yesterday's Advertiser that the Japanese boxer Yamogata who arrived last week from Seattle would probably make his debut at the Athletic Park next Saturday afternoon.

It is only quite recently that Japan has started to figure on the boxing map and Yamogata is the first Nipponese battler to come to Honolulu.

Yujiro Watanabe and Young Togo have performed well in the mainland rings and the fame of their doings has spread to Hawaii. Togo, indeed, was to have visited Honolulu and boxed here and undoubtedly would have done so had it not been for the mysterious affliction which overtook him when he was in the ring with Roy Moore at Oakland six weeks ago.

Yamogata has had twenty fights in the neighborhood of Seattle and has never been defeated. He is said to be rugged and game and to possess a fair share of cleverness and a punch which has put an opponent to sleep on several occasions.

Bill Prestidge is looking after Yamogata and says that from what he has seen of him he will do. Prestidge has had a long and varied experience with boxers and wrestlers and his opinion on the merits of the Jap is worth while.

The matter of whether Yamogata will box on Saturday next will be definitely settled today. If he is signed up it will be for a four-round bout, probably with "Plug" Milne.

The Training Schedule.

All the boxers engaged in the coming carnival took matters easily yesterday, nothing more strenuous than roadwork being done.

This afternoon at three o'clock at Camp Very Ben de Mello will spar with Corporal Trier and other volunteers who may present themselves.

At 5:30 Young Caples will work at the Orpheum with Johnny McCarthy, and at the same place Ingle and Young Gans will box with Milne, Kid Herrigan, Greene, McCarhty, et al.

The ring at the Athletic Park will be erected over the home plate and will be raised a sufficient distance from the ground to ensure everybody in the grandstand and bleachers having a clear view of the proceedings.

The sun, after four o'clock is behind the grandstand and the light will be excellent for principals and spectators alike.

Arrangements are being made to handle three thousand people and no effort will be spared to ensure the comfort of every patron.

The question of referee has not yet been decided, but will be settled in a day or two. If Johnny McCarthy will consent to act it is probable that he will be third man in the ring, for it is understood that he is agreeable to both parties.

Today Determines if Yamogata Will Box Saturday

Great interest was created among the local Japanese by the announcement in yesterday's Advertiser that the Japanese boxer Yamogata who arrived last week from Seattle would probably make his debut at the Athletic Park next Saturday afternoon. It is only quite recently that Japan has started to figure on the boxing map and Yamogata is the first Nipponese battler to come to Honolulu.

Yujiro Watanabe and Young Togo have performed well in the mainland rings and the fame of their doings has spread to Hawaii.

Togo, indeed, was to have visited Honolulu and boxed here and undoubtedly would have done so had it not been for the mysterious affliction which overtook him when he was in the ring with Roy Moore at Oakland six weeks ago.

Yamogata has had twenty fights in the neighborhood of Seattle and has never been defeated. He is said to be rugged and game and to possess a fair share of cleverness and a punch which has put an opponent to sleep on several occasions.

Bill Prestidge is looking after Yamogata and says that from what he has seen of him he will do. Prestidge has had a long and varied experience with boxers and wresters and his opinion of the merits of the Jap is worth while (sic.)

The matter of whether Yamogata will box on Saturday next will be definitely settled today. If he is signed up it will be for a four-round bout, probably with "Plug" Milne.

The Training Schedule

All the boxers engaged in the coming carnival took matters easily yesterday, nothing more strenuous than roadwork being done. This afternoon at three o'clock at Camp Very Ben de Mello will spar with Corporal Trier and other volunteers who may present themselves.

At 5:30 Young Caples will work at the Orpheum with Johnny McCarthy, and at the same place Ingel and Young Gans will box with Milne, Kid Herrigan, Greene, McCarthy, et al.

The ring at the Athletic Park will be erected over the home plate and will be raised a sufficient distance from the ground to ensure everybody in the grandstand and bleachers having a clear view of the proceedings.

The sun, after four o'clock is behind the grandstand and the light will be excellent for principals and spectators alike.

Arrangements are being made to handle three thousand people and no effort will be spared to ensure the comfort of every patron.

The question of referee has not yet been decided, but will be settled in a day or two. If johnny McCarthy will consent to act it is probable that he will be third man in the ring, for it is understood that he is agreeable to both parties.

February 19th 1921 Chicago Eagle

Yujiro Watanabe to Establish School and Will Import American Boxers for Exhibitions.

Japan soon will flourish as a boxing center, according to Yujiro Watanabe, Japanese boxer, who is on his way to Tokyo to establish a boxing school. He will also have a school at Osaka and will import American boxers for exhibitions later, he said.

Yujiro Watanabe to Establish School and Will Import American Boxers for Exhibitions

Japan soon will flourish as a boxing center, according to Yujiro Watanabe, Japanese boxer, who is on his way to Tokyo to establish a boxing school at Osaka and will import American boxers for exhibitions later, he said.

January 21st 1921 The San Francisco Examiner

LAND OF THE CHERRY BLOSSOM TO TRY HAND AT BOXING

By BILL YEAGER

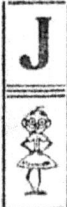

JAPAN is soon to blossom forth as a boxing center. The land of jiu-jitsu and wrestling is taking to the sport and already a number of American and English instructors are teaching the young generation how to use their "dukes" as a means of defense.

Yesterday Yujiro Watanabe, who will be remembered by the boxing fans of 1909 when he was setting the four round ranks on fire with his battling, arrived in town. Watanabe fought Willie Hoppe when the latter was in his prime and was one of the few men who ever knocked the terror off his feet.

Watanabe was beaten here by Dick Wayne for the first time in his career. He fought practically every tough lightweight on the coast during his stay around here and was considered the lightweight champion of the Pacific for some months.

Watanabe is leaving Saturday for Japan. He will go direct to Tokio and there establish a boxing school for the natives. He has several letters written him from influential Japanese who have offered to back him in the venture and furnish him with a place to hold boxing bouts.

The Jap boxer has been in Salt Lake in charge of a number of concessions on the big pier there and after leaving there he went to the mines in Colorado, where he worked alongside of Hashimura Togo Koriyama, another Japanese boxer who has shown here.

Watanabe intends to import several American boxers and trainers if he finds that the sport will take among his native people. He will also establish a boxing school in Osaka, a thriving town near Tokio. He will remain in Japan long enough to give the sport a good footing and then come back here to induce American fighters to go back with him.

108

Land of the Cherry Blossom to Try Hand at Boxing
By Bill Yeager

Japan is soon to blossom forth as a boxing center. The land of jiu-jitsu and wrestling is taking to the sport and already a number of American and English instructors are teaching the younger generation how to use their "dukes" as a means of defense.

Yesterday Yujiro Watanabe, who will be remembered by the boxing fans of 1909 when he was setting the four round ranks on fire with his battling, arrived in town. Watanabe fought Willie Hoppe when the latter was in his prime and was one of the few men who ever knocked the terror off his feet.

Watanabe was beaten here by Dick Wayne for the first time in his career. He fought practically every tough lightweight on the coast during his stay around here and was considered the lightweight champion of the Pacific for some months. Watanabe is leaving Saturday for Japan. He will go direct to Tokio (sic) and there establish a boxing school for the natives. He has several letters written him from influential Japanese who have offered to back him in the venture and furnish him with a place to hold boxing bouts.

The Jap boxer has been in Salt Lake in charge of a number of concessions on the big pier there and after leaving there he went to the mines in Colorado, where he worked alongside of Hashimura Togo Koriyama, another Japanese boxer who has shown here.

Watanabe intends to import several American boxers and trainers if he finds that the sport will take among his native people. He will also establish a boxing school in Osaka, a thriving town near Tokio. He will remain in Japan long enough to give the sport a good footing and then come back here to induce American fighters to go back with him.

May 6th 1922 Asahi Newspaper

△拳闘試合

Kento Shiai

Boxing Matches Featuring Americans vs Japanese. The Americans are Young Churchill and Spider Rocche, the Japanese are Young Togo and Watanabe Yujiro of the Japanese Boxing Club. The matches will take place at the Sumo training facility within Yasukuni Shrine in the Kudanshita area of Tokyo at 2pm tomorrow, May 7th rain or shine.

February 10th 1923 Asahi Newspaper

酒と煙草は禁物の拳闘練習
戸山學校ではじめる

Sake and Tobacco not allowed when training boxing
Training starts at the Toyama School

Having seen a demonstration of boxing by the Japan Boxing Club the administration of Toyama School, General Mitamura, was impressed. He commented, "I couldn't take my eyes away," and "I was hooked!" The General invited the instructor Watanabe Yujiro to demonstrate boxing techniques before 200 students. There is a plan to begin a boxing program at the school, however Watanabe cautioned, "For a boxer the three things you have to keep away from are women, Sake and tobacco!"

Watanabe is on the right and General Mitamura is in the center.

110

December 17ᵗʰ 1927 Lancaster New Era (Pennsylvania)

Professor Yujiro Watanabe, an old time boxer, known as the father of boxing in Japan, has invited Jack Dempsey to come to Tokio. The professor teaches boxing in two universities and assured Dempsey that the people will come from miles around to see him.

December 12ᵗʰ 1927 The Tampa Tribune

Japan Wants To See Dempsey Step

SAN FRANCISCO, Dec. 11.—(A.P.) —Japanese have heard much of the feats of Jack Dempsey and would like to see in person the former heavy-weight champion, who has been pictured in some remote parts of the country as an eight-foot giant with flowing side whiskers.

Professor Yujiro Watanabe, who fought here years ago and is known as the father of boxing in Japan, extended the invitation. Watanabe, now a teacher of boxing in two universities in Tokyo, assures Mr. Dempsey that "people will come from miles around to see him."

June 21st 1928
Asahi Newspaper

けん闘選手の出發
（右より臼田岡本選手、渡雄監督）

けん闘選手
出發
昨夜津田選
手と共に

Boxers Depart
On the right side are the boxers Masuda and Okamaoto.
On the left is Coach Watanabe.

Boxers Depart Last Night
Our Olympic athletes set out for the 28th Olympiad in Netherlands.

June 26th 1931 Asahi Newspaper

American Boxers Visit Japan
Arrived in Yokohama Last Night on the Ship Tatsuda Maru

Three fighters John Ozonel[28], Dan Levy and Pavolini were invited to Japan and arrived abord the Tatsuda Maru on the 25th in Yokohama. Mr. Watanabe Yujiro who accompanied the reporter explained,

Ozonel is flyweight and is famous for going ten rounds with Paburodano. I am hoping to use him as a barometer to test my fighters abilities. Levey has been boxing for ten years. In 1925 he became the Navy's Feather Division Champion. In 1927 he fought the famous boxer Golia and has a record of one victory and one loss against him.

Pavolini has an impressive record though it is not as good as the previous fellow's, he fought 75 times but has never been knocked out. Boxing fans in Japan will be 100% impressed with their spirit. The plan is to start on July 3rd in the Hibiya, Tokyo training hall. They will be in various competitions over the next two months.

---

[28] It is difficult to determine the correct spelling for these fighter's names since they are rendered in the Japanese Katakana alphabet. The spellings are my best guess.

March 10th 1932
The Press Democrat (Santa Rosa, California)

Yujiro Watanabe, without a doubt the best Japanese fighter developed so far, who battled Willie Ritchie and Willie Hoppe, and all the others of that time, is back in Tokyo, where he runs a fight club and instructs students in boxing at one of the universities. He is a "professor" now.

Yujiro Watanabe, without a doubt the best Japanese fighter developed so far, who battled Willie Ritchie and Willie Hoppe, and all the others of that time, is back in Tokyo, where he runs a fight club and instructs students in boxing at one of the universities. He is a "professor" now.

June 6th 1934
News Pilot San Pedro, California

TOMMY TRIMMED

Professor Yujiro Watanabe, who introduced boxing to Japan, writes from Tokyo, and this will surprise western fight fans, that Young Tommy, star Filipino bantamweight took a licking from "Horiguchi" May 1. It was a ten rounder. Tommy has a habit of beating about every boy he meets and is one of our top-rankers. Horiguchi is one of the most popular fighters in Japan. Some 30,000 fans, accounting for the biggest gate ever drawn in Japan, turned out. Watanabe fought the leading light-weights around here 20 years ago.

Tommy Trimmed

Professor Yujiro Watanabe, who introduced boxing to Japan, writes from Tokyo, and this will surprise western fight fans, that Young Tommy, star Filipino bantamweight took a licking from "Horiguchi" May 1. It was a ten rounder. Tommy has a habit of beating about every boy he meets and is one of our top rankers. Horiguchi is one of the most popular fighters in Japan. Some 30,000 fans, accounting for the biggest gate ever drawn in Japan turned out. Watanabe fought the leading lightweights around here 20 years ago.

Obituary
June 29th 1956

渡辺勇次郎氏（元日本洋拳倶楽部会長）肝臓ガンのため二十八日夜東京目黒の国立第二病院で死去、六十八歳。日本に初めてボクシングを紹介した人。その門弟に岡本不二、中村金雄、笹崎僙、ピストン堀口選手らがいた。

Mr. Watanabe Yujiro (Formerly the president of the Japan Boxing Club) died of liver cancer on the night of the 28th at Number Two Tokyo Meguro National Hospital. He was the first to introduce boxing to Japan. Some of his students were Okamoto Fuji, Nakamura Kaneo, Sasazaki Ko and Piston Horiguchi.

Koriyama Kokichi "Young Togo"
23 Bouts 3 Wins (2 KO) 11 Loss 5 Draw
Source: Boxrec

JAP PUNCHSWAPPERS WHO WILL FIGHT EASTERN PUGS

YOUNG TOGO AND YOUNG OYAMA

Koriyama Kokichi : Author

There is not a lot of biographical information about Koriyama Kokichi. He was born in 1887 and went to America in 1907. Over the course of his boxing career he earned various nicknames including "Young Togo" "Jap Togo" and "The Yellow Peril." His height is given as 4′ 10″ or 147cm. It is not clear when he met his co-author Watanabe.

Interestingly, there were two Japanese boxers active in America in the early 20th century nicknamed "Young Togo." I was able to locate numerous articles and pictures of "Young Togo," however it was not clear which of the men was the co-author of this book.

"Togo" refers to Marshal-Admiral the Marquis Togo Hihachiro 東郷平八郎 (1848 ~ 1934.) At the time he was the head of the Japanese Navy. He was famous for leading the Japanese Navy to overwhelming victory over the Russian pacific fleet in 1905, thereby becoming one of Japan's greatest naval heroes.

Left: A portrait of Admiral Togo. Right: A 1904 political cartoon showing Admiral Togo standing over the defeated Russian Pacific fleet as the Russian Baltic fleet approaches. The Baltic fleet would be crushed in 1905.

ONLY WAITING

THE CZAR'S BALTIC FLEET IS ENROUTE TO THE FAR EAST.—NEWS ITEM.

December 13th 1907 The Los Angeles Times

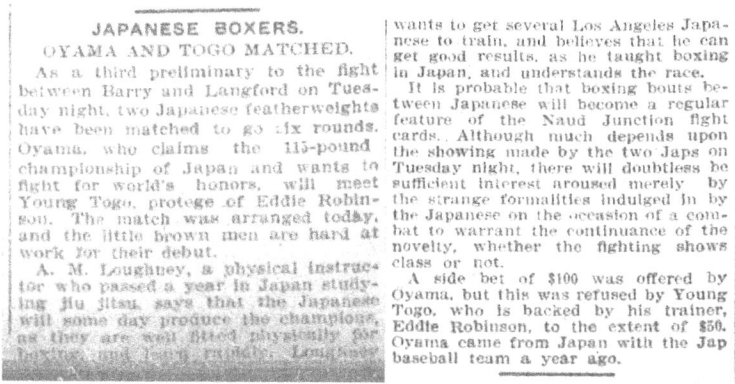

JAPANESE BOXERS.

OYAMA AND TOGO MATCHED.

As a third preliminary to the fight between Barry and Langford on Tuesday night, two Japanese featherweights have been matched to go six rounds. Oyama, who claims the 115-pound championship of Japan and wants to fight for world's honors, will meet Young Togo, protege of Eddie Robinson. The match was arranged today, and the little brown men are hard at work for their debut.

A. M. Loughney, a physical instructor who passed a year in Japan studying jiu jitsu, says that the Japanese will some day produce the champions, as they are well fitted physically for boxing and learn rapidly. Loughney

wants to get several Los Angeles Japanese to train, and believes that he can get good results, as he taught boxing in Japan, and understands the race.

It is probable that boxing bouts between Japanese will become a regular feature of the Naud Junction fight cards. Although much depends upon the showing made by the two Japs on Tuesday night, there will doubtless be sufficient interest aroused merely by the strange formalities indulged in by the Japanese on the occasion of a combat to warrant the continuance of the novelty, whether the fighting shows class or not.

A side bet of $100 was offered by Oyama, but this was refused by Young Togo, who is backed by his trainer, Eddie Robinson, to the extent of $50. Oyama came from Japan with the Jap baseball team a year ago.

Japanese Boxers
Oyama and Togo Matched

As a third preliminary to the fight between Barry and Langford on Tuesday night, two Japanese featherweights have been matched to go six rounds. Oyama, who claims the 115-pound championship of Japan and wants to fight for the world's honors, will meet Young Togo, protégé of Eddie Robinson. The match was arranged today and the little brown men are hard at work for their debut.

A.M. Loughney, a physical instructor who passed a year in Japan studying jiu jitsu, says that the Japanese will someday produce the champions as they are well fitted physically for boxing and learn rapidly

Loughney wants to get several Los Angeles Japanese to train, and believes that he can get good results, as he taught boxing in Japan, and understands the race.

It is probable that boxing bouts between Japanese will become a regular feature of the Naud Junction fight cards. Although much depends upon the showing made by the two Japs on Tuesday night, there will doubtless be sufficient interest aroused merely by the strange formalities indulged in by the Japanese on the occasion of a combat to warrant the continuance of the novelty, whether the fighting shows class or not.

A side bet of $100 was offered by Oyama, but this was refused by Young Togo, who is backed by his trainer, Eddie Robinson, to the extent of $50. Oyama came from Japan with the Jap baseball team a year ago.

December 18th 1907 Los Angeles Evening Post-Record

> Young Togo and Young Oyama
> furnished the chief amusement of
> the evening. They lambasted each
> other for six rounds and had the
> crowd shrieking during the entire
> time. Both subjects of the Mikado
> were willing, but their chief trou-
> ble lay in a lack of knowledge as
> to what their hands were for.
> They pawed at each other and
> failing to land would use a jiu jitsu
> stunt. But the crowd liked it and
> that sufficed. Togo was awarded
> the decision.

Young Togo and Young Oyama furnished the chief amusement of the evening. They lambasted each other for six rounds and had the crowd shrieking during the entire time. Both subjects of the Mikado were willing, but their chief trouble lay in a lack of knowledge as to what their hands were for.

They pawed at each other and failing to land would use a jiu jitsu stunt. But the crowd liked it and that sufficed. Togo was awarded the decision.

December 10th 1907 Los Angeles Times

> It is also probable that Young Togo
> and Young Oyama, the two Japanese
> fighters, who went six rounds on Mon-
> day night, will be matched again. They
> surprised the fight fans with their
> showing, and Young Togo, the winner
> of the bout, was talked of as a possi-
> ble opponent of Young McGovern, but
> McCarey says he will not match the
> Japs against a white boy until they
> have studied the game for several
> months more.

It is also probable that Young Togo and Young Oyama, the two Japanese fighters, who went six rounds on Monday night, will be matched again. They surprised the fight fans with their showing, and Young Togo, the winner of the bout, was talked of as a possible opponent of Young McGovern, but McCarey says he will not match the Japs against a white boy until they have studied the game for several months more.

June 21ˢᵗ 1908 The Los Angeles Times

Japs to Give Another Bout in Tonight's Card.

The first preliminary, between the Japs, will be another slam-bang affair, such as won great favor with the fans when Young Togo and Oyama fought. Oyama, who meets Kuroki tonight, lost in his first battle and will endeavor to beat his opponent in order to get another chance with the little scrapper who beat him.

Japs to Give Another Bout in Tonight's Card

The first preliminary, between the Japs, will be another slam-bang affair, such as won great favor with the fans when Young Togo and Oyama fought. Oyama, who meets Kuroki tonight, lost in his first battle and will endeavor to beat his opponent in order to get another chance with the little scrapper who beat him.

March 6ᵗʰ 1917 Oakland Tribune

GOOD SHOW AT CLEAVER'S.
The rest of the card will bring together some good boys. Herb Brodie and Walter McDevitt, the fighting barber, will get together; Tommy Hayes meets Togo Koriyama, the Japanese crackerjack; while Henry Hendricks and Roy Tabor will try to rock each other to sleep. Kid

Good Show At Cleaver's

The rest of the card will bring together some good boys. Herb Brodie and Walter McDevitt, the fighting barber, will get together; Tommy Hayes meets Togo Koriyama, the Japanese crackerjack; while Henry Hendricks and Roy Tabor will try to rock each other to sleep.

May 25th 1908 The Shreveport Journal (Shreveport, Louisiana)

Los Angeles, May 25.—A Japanese fighter, who is also a jiu jitsu man, has made his appearance among the local scrappers and, having cleaned up many lights of the "prelim" class, has announced his intention of invading the eastern states in search of glory and gold.

He is Young Togo of Tokio. He has been in this country about three years, but has been fihting for only six months. His style is something brand new.

Instead of trying to protect himself he walks into almost any kind of a punch and goes down repeatedly. He stays only a second, and then comes to his feet with a spring, prepared to take some more punches in order to land one.

The first time Togo fought here he was regarded as a joke. He was battered around the ring for several rounds and the spectators were becoming disgusted when Togo suddenly straightened and put his man out with a solar plexus blow. The knockout came like a flash. There were few who saw the blow land.

Young Togo of Tokio Cleans up Many in "Prelim" Class in San Francisco

Los Angeles, May 25. A Japanese fighter, who is also a jiu jitsu man, has made his appearance among the local scrappers and, having cleaned up many lights of the "prelim" class, has announced his intention of invading the eastern states in search of glory and gold.

He is Young Togo of Tokio. He has been in this country about three years, but has been fighting for only six months. His style is something brand new.

Instead of trying to protect himself he walked into almost any kind of a punch and goes down repeatedly. He stays only a second, and then comes to his feet with a spring, prepared to take some more punches in order to land one.

The first time Togo fought here he was regarded as a joke. He was battered around the ring for several rounds and the spectators were becoming disgusted when Togo suddenly straightened and put his man out with a solar plexus blow. The knockout came like a flash. There were few who saw the blow land.

September 7th 1908 The Evening Mail (Stockton California)

Togo Beaten in the Preliminary Near Los Angeles.

VERNON, Los Angeles, September 7.—By 2:05 p. m. the galleries of the great pavilion were filled to the last seat with 1500 persons closely packed.

Jimmy Austin and Young Togo, a Jap, were scheduled for an eight-round go. The gong sounded a moment later for the preliminary, and the little fellows went at each other vigorously. The crowd was set wild by the slugging. Togo is the first Jap fighter ever seen in this city and his work was watched with interest. He showed much boxing ability. The first round was even.

JAP DEFEATED.

The referee gave the decision to Austin after eight rounds of fighting. This was unpopular with the crowd, who cheered the Jap as he left the ring.

Togo Beaten in the Preliminary Near Los Angeles

Vernon, Los Angeles, September 7- By 2:05 pm the galleries of the great pavilion were filled to the last seat with 1500 persons closely packed.

Jimmy Austin and Young Togo, a Jap, were scheduled for an eight-round go. The gong sounded a moment later for the preliminary, and the little fellows went at each other vigorously. The crowd was set wild by the slugging. Togo is the first Japanese fighter ever seen in this city and his work was watched with interest. He showed much boxing ability. The first round was even.

Jap Defeated

The referee gave the decision to Austin after eight rounds of fighting. This was unpopular with the crowd, who cheered the Jap as he left the ring.

April 11th 1909
The Baltimore Sun

Jap Punchswappers Who Will Fight Eastern Pugs

JAP PUNCHSWAPPERS WHO WILL FIGHT EASTERN PUGS

YOUNG TOGO AND YOUNG OYAMA

Young Togo and Young Oyama

May 8th 1909
The Tacoma Times

YELLOW PERIL THREATENS THE EASTERN PRIZE RINGS

LOS ANGELES, Cal., May 7.—Fight fans of the East will soon have an opportunity of seeing two real Japanese boxers in action who can certainly handle themselves with all the manners of a topnotch pugilist. The yellow boys are Young Oyama and Young Togo, 133 and 105 pounders respectively. The Japs are planning an invasion of the East this summer and hope to return to their native land with the scalps of many American boxers hanging at their belts.

The Japs fight as do no other race in the world. Their principal asset is gameness, combined with only a fair amount of cleverness. Oyama is the cleverer of the two, and when he fights his saffron-colored skin contracts until it is drawn tight over the bones of the face, giving him the appearance of his satanic majesty. Oyama is a perfect demon, never stopping from the time the bell sounds to start the fight until it is over.

Just the reverse is Young Togo. He fights with a continual grin face. He never appears to be serious, yet has a knack of winning his battles. His first fight here nearly resulted in a riot. He was knocked down in the first round just ten times, yet, in the very next session, he came on and whipped his opponent, dropping him in the middle of the second.

The Japs will leave this city in a few days and expect to be gone about six months, traveling through the East and fighting in every city where there is a boxing club—provided, of course, that matches can be secured.

Yellow Peril Threatens The Eastern Prize Rings

Los Angeles, Cal., May 7. -Fight fans of the East will soon have an opportunity of seeing two real Japanese boxers in action who can certainly handle themselves with all the manners of a topnotch pugilist. The yellow boys are Young Oyama and Young Togo, 133 and 105 pounders respectively. The Japs are planning an invasion of the East this summer and hope to return to their native land with the scalps of many American boxers hanging at their belts.

The Japs fight as do no other race in the world. Their principal asset is gameness, combined with only a fair amount of cleverness. Oyama is the cleverer of the two, and when he fights his saffron-colored skin contracts until it is drawn tight over the bones of the face, giving him the appearance of his satanic majesty. Oyama is a perfect demon, never stopping from the time the bell sounds to start the fight until it is over.

Just the reverse is Young Togo. He fights with a continual grin face. He never appears to be serious, yet has a knack of winning his battles. His first fight here nearly resulted in a riot. He was knocked down in the first round just ten times, yet, in the very next session, he came out and whipped his opponent, dropping him in the middle of the second.

The Japs will leave this city in a few days and expect to be gone about six months, travelling through the east and fighting in every city where there is a boxing club – provided, of course, that matches can be secured.

June 18th 1910
The Oregon Daily Journal

YOUNG TOGO SAYS NO SLEEP PILLS

Bennett Will Have No Chance to Send Him to Land of Nod.

Young Togo, the diminutive Jap wrestler who meets Jockey Bennett, a boxer, and "Abby" Abernathy, a wrestler in the same night, agreeing to subdue both of them, is one of the best examples of physical development among the Japanese in Portland. He has a splendid physique and is able to withstand all sorts of punishment.

A discussion came up this morning as to what chance Bennett has of winning the mixed match. If Bennett happens to clip the Nippon on the inferior maxillary, and the almond-orbed boy from the orient goes down for the count of ten, it will be curtains with him.

According to the best brand of information Eddie Robinson gives out, this will be an impossibility. He says the Jap has never yet heard the twittering of the birdies and Bennett is not the lad who can bounce an alfalfa producer off his knob.

When the trio goes on the mat next Friday night in Merrill's hall, Abernathy will tackle the Jap first and Bennett will figure in the windup. Four Japanese jiu jitsu wrestlers, one of whom is from Seattle, will furnish the preliminaries.

Young Togo Says No Sleep Pills
Bennett Will Have No Chance to Send Him to Land of Nod

Young Togo, the diminutive Japanese wrestler who meets Jockey Bennett, a boxer, and "Abby" Abernathy, a wrestler in the same night, agreeing to subdue both of them, is one of the best examples of physical development among the Japanese in Portland. He has a splendid physique and is able to withstand all sorts of punishment.

A discussion came up this morning as to what chance Bennett has of winning the mixed match. If Bennett happens to clip the Nippon on the inferior maxillary, and the almond-orbed boy from the orient goes down for the count of ten, it will be curtains with him.

According to the best brand of information, Eddie Robinson gives out, this will be an impossibility. He says the Jap has never yet heard the twittering of the birdies and Bennett is not the lad who can bounce an alfalfa producer off his knob.

When the trio goes on the mat next Friday night in Merrill's hall, Aberthany will tackle the Jap first and Bennett will figure in the windup. Four Japanese jiu jitsu wrestlers, one of whom is from Seattle, will furnish the preliminaries.

September 30th 1910 The Daily Oklahoman

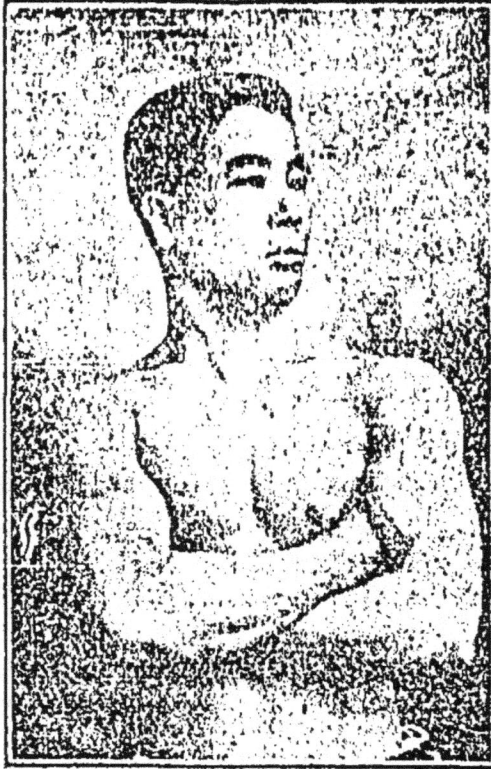

IN JIU JITSU

Young Togo is slated to meet a good welterweight in a test of American wrestling vs. Jiu Jitsu at the Lyric theatre next Thursday night. Prior to that date, Togo will travel over the state meeting all who desire to go against him.

In Jiu Jitsu

Young Togo is slated to meet a good welterweight in a test of American wrestling vs. Jiu Jitsu at the Lyric theater next Thursday night. Prior to that date, Togo will travel over the state meeting all who desire to go against him.

December 20th 1910
Sapulpa Evening Light (Oklahoma)

YOUNG TOGO, "THE LITTLE DEMON."

Young Togo, "The Little Demon."

July 5th 1911
The Brooklyn Citizen

THIS JAP IS SOME FIGHTER.

Young Togo Goes Fifteen Rounds with Harry Forbes.

McVALESTER, Okla., July 5.— Young Togo, a full-blooded Japanese boy, today is hailed as a coming bantam champion by those who yesterday saw him stand shoulder to shoulder with Harry Forbes, the "come back" champion, and exchange blows for fifteen rounds without giving in.

Forbes outweighed him nearly ten pounds.

This Jap is Some Fighter
Young Togo Goes Fifteen Rounds With Harry Forbes

McValester, Okla. July 5
Young Togo, a full-blooded Japanese boy, today is hailed as a coming bantam champion by those who yesterday saw him stand shoulder to shoulder with Harry Forbes, the "comeback" champion and exchange blows for fifteen rounds without giving in. Forbes outweighed him nearly ten pounds.

May 12th 1912
Oakland Tribune

YOUNG TOGO IS GOING BLIND AND WILL HAVE BENEFIT

SAN FRANCISCO, May 11.—A testimonial benefit will be tendered Young Togo, the Japanese featherweight pugilist, who has lost the sight of one eye and is threatened with total blindness, by his countrymen and admirers at Dreamland Rink on Wednesday evening, May 15. Young Togo's eye trouble is said to be incurable and a series of interesting athletic events have been carded for his benefit.

Willie Ritchie, Frankie Burns, Eddie Campl; Roy Moore and a number of other well known local boxers will appear, and in addition there will be jiu jitsu versus catch-as-catch-can wrestling bouts and there will be the regular jiu jitsu contests. The price of admission will be from 25 cents to $1.

Young Togo is Going Blind And Will Have Benefit

San Francisco, May 11.- A testimonial benefit will be tendered Young Togo, the Japanese featherweight pugilist, who has lost the sight of one eye and is threatened with total blindness, by his countrymen and admirers at Dreamland Rink on Wednesday evening, May 15th. Young Togo's eye trouble is said to be incurable and a series of interesting athletic events have been carded for his benefit.

Willie Ritchie, Frankie Burns, Eddie Campl; Roy Moore and a number of other well-known local boxers will appear in addition there will be jiu jitsu versus catch-as-catch-can wrestling bouts and there will be the regular jiu jitsu contests. The price of admission will be from 25 cents to 1$.

May 12ᵗʰ 1912 The San Francisco Call

YOUNG TOGO is a finished fighter. He is a Japanese boy, who took the name of his country's admiral, who is somewhat of a fighting man himself, in a different medium.

Young Togo fought until his eyes were out; literally, he was beaten into blindness—finished. He is to be given a benefit at the Dreamland pavilion next Wednesday evening. He was produced at the Howard street ring side yesterday by Announcer Billy Jordan, while the benefit was announced.

Stumbling behind dark glasses, the Japanese fighting boy was led into the dark ring.

"Young Togo, who is going blind," said Jordan. "There will be a benefit entertainment for him at Dreamland on next Wednesday."

The smoked ivory boy was being led from the ring, when some one from a box seat slyly tossed a dollar into the ring. It was followed by another dollar, by a half, by a quarter—dollars, halves and quarters sailed through the air. A theatrical man passed up a $10 bill. The ring retainers were busy for several minutes collecting the money. There was a hatful for the little Togo to weigh and count.

Young Togo is a finished fighter. He is a Japanese boy, who took the name of his country's admiral, who is somewhat of a fighting man himself, in a different medium.

Young Togo fought until his eyes were out: literally, he was beaten into blindness-finished. He is to be given a benefit at the Dreamland pavilion next Wednesday evening. He was produced at the Howard street ring side yesterday by Announcer Billy Jordan, while the benefit was announced.

Stumbling behind dark glasses, the Japanese fighting boy was led into the dark ring.

"Young Togo, who is going blind," said Jordan. "There will be a benefit entertainment for him at Dreamland on next Wednesday."

The smoked ivory boy was being led from the ring, when someone from a box seat slyly tossed a dollar into the ring. It was followed by another dollar, by a half, by a quarter-dollars, halves and quarters sailed through the air. A theatrical man passed up a $10 bill. The ring retainers were busy for several minutes collecting the money. There was a hatful for the little Togo to weigh and count.

July 7th 1912 Honolulu Advertiser

> At the recent Dreamland Park bene-
> fit to the Japanese pugilist, in San
> Francisco, a fellow countryman of his
> appeared in one of the preliminaries,
> but, as a coast paper says, "Yujiro
> Watanabe, a Japanese, caught a tartar
> in Willie Hoppe, and in the third
> round, after being practically slaught-
> ered, the referee stopped the fight and
> raised Hoppe's glove."

> Young Togo, the Japanese boxer,
> who is totally blind in one eye and
> whose other optic is on the verge of
> going sideless, was tendered a testi-
> monial benefit at Dreamland Pavilion
> in San Francisco by his countrymen
> and friends. As quite a number of
> prominent members of the fistic pro-
> fession volunteered their services for
> the occasion, there was a big outpour-
> ing of the regulars.
> Togo fought ten hard rounds in his
> present condition at the West Oak-
> land Club, and ever since that night he
> has been under the care of a physician.

At the recent Dreamland Park benefit to the Japanese pugilist, in San Francisco, a fellow countryman of his appeared in one of the preliminaries, but, as a coast paper says, "Yujiro Watanabe, a Japanese, caught a Tartar[29] in Willie Hoppe, and in the third round, after being practically slaughtered, the referee stopped the fight and raised Hoppe's glove."

Young Togo, the Japanese boxer, who is totally blind in one eye and whose other optic is on the verge of going sightless, was tendered a testimonial benefit at Dreamland Pavilion in san Francisco by his countrymen and friends. As quite a number of prominent members of the fistic profession volunteered their services for the occasion, there was a big outpouring of the regulars.

Togo fought ten hard rounds in his present condition at the West Oakland Club, and ever since that night he has been under the care of a physician.

---

[29] "Catch a Tartar" means to seek out someone that turns out to be unexpectedly formidable. Refers to Turkic or Mongolian invaders of Asia in the Middle Ages.

April 22nd 1922 Stockton Daily Evening Record

JAP BOXER RETURNS TO MOTHERLAND

[United Press.]

SAN FRANCISCO, April 22. — Togo Koriyama, Japanese-American lightweight pugilist, who has gained some fame in Southern California, is en route to the Flowery Isles to stage some bouts with his jui-jitsu fellow-countrymen who have idfferent ideas on the subject of just what constitutes the manly art of self defense.

"Moose" Taussig, nationally known manager and trainer, is taking over a collection of pugs with him to pioneer the fight game in the Mikado's kingdom. "Spider" Roach, San Francisco lightweight; Young Ketchell, Los Angeles welterweight, and Togo compose his party. He isn't taking any heavyweights, fearing that it would be a waste of time in the island of little men.

The big promoter in Japan is Yujiro Watanabe, a prominent lightweight in the four-round game 10 years ago. Wanatabe,fought many good 133-pounders, including Willie Ritchie. The American party will remain in the islands for several months.

Jap Boxer Returns to Motherland

United Press.San Francisco, April 22. – Togo Koriyama, Japanese-American lightweight pugilist, who has gained some fame in Southern California, is en route to the Flowery Isles to stage some bouts with his jiu-jitsu fellow-countrymen who have different ideas on the subject of just what constitutes the many art of self-defense.

"Moose" Taussig, nationally known manager and trainer is taking over a collection of pugs with him to pioneer the fight game in the Mikado's kingdom. "Spider" Roach, San Francisco lightweight: Young Ketchell, Los Angeles welterweight, and Togo compose his party. He isn't taking any heavyweights, fearing that it would be a waste of time in the island of little men.

The big promoter in Japan is Yujiro Watanabe, a prominent lightweight in the four-round game 10 years ago. Watanabe fought many good 133-pounders, including Willie Ritchie. The American party will remain in the islands for several months.

June 1ˢᵗ 1925
Times Herald (Olean, New York)

"Tin Ears" Now Modish As Japan Takes Up Boxing

By LUTHER A. HUSTON,
International News Service Staff Correspondent

Tokyo, June 1—However widespread depression may be in other lines of business in Japan, the "cauliflower" industry is flourishing. The crop of "tin ears" is not threatened by a shortage.

Which is to say that Japan is developing pugilistic ambitions and has begun to train her husky youths in the science, art or pastime of administering effectively the soporific wallop. In still other words, Japan now is beginning to take up boxing in a serious way in the hope of developing a few sockers capable of competing with those of other lands. There are even some Japanese who indulge in the pleasant and harmless pastime of hoping that one day Nippon will produce a world's champion.

Good Outlook

The nestor of Japanese boxing is Togo Koriyama, who knocked about the world for seventeen years, mostly in the United States, allowing scrappers of many lands to work over his features in the most approved fistic fashion. He has acquired a beautiful pair of demoralized ears, and his nose has been knocked askew in artistic fashion. Now he has undertaken to teach his young countrymen the tricks he learned.

"Tin Ears[30]" Now Modish As Japan Takes Up Boxing
By Luther A. Huston
International News Service Staff Correspondent

Tokyo, June 1 – However widespread depression may be in other lines of business in Japan, the "cauliflower" industry is flourishing.

The crop of "tin ears" is not threatened by a shortage.

Which is to say that Japan is developing pugilistic ambitions and has begun to train her husky youths in the science, art or pastime of administering effectively the soporific[31] wallop. In still other words, Japan now is beginning to take up boxing in a serious way in hope of developing a few sockers capable of competing with those of other lands. There are even some Japanese who indulge in the pleasant and harmless pastime of hoping that one day Nippon will produce a world's champion.

Good Outlook

The nestor of Japanese boxing is Togo Koriyama, who knocked about the world for seventeen years, mostly in the United States, allowing scrappers of many lands to work over his features in the most approved fistic fashion. He has acquired a beautiful pair of demoralized ears, and his nose has been knocked askew in artistic fashion. Now he has undertaken to teach his young countrymen the tricks learned.

---

[30] From: Prize Fighters Disdain "Tin Ears," Most Boxers, However, Get Those Ears. El Paso Texas Herald Jan 14th 1916:

About eight out of every ten fist fighters you see nowadays own the "cauliflower," or "tin" ear; an ear so battered and punched by the bludgeonings of five-ounce gloves that it isn't really an ear any more at all, but just a misshapen chunk of cartilage clinging to the side of the head.

[31] Soporific - Causing sleep or making a person want to sleep.

Koriyama has an adequately equipped gymnasium at Mikage, where he conducts the Japan Boxing Association. According to Koriyama the raw material from which he hopes to harvest his crop of champions is decidedly promising.

There is one stalwart youth in Koriyama's camp of whom he is especially proud. He is known as "Fighting' Otora.

"That boy has a wallop that would make the heart of Dempsey rejoice," Koriyama declared. "I really think that, when he has learned a little more about the game, Otora will be able to make things interesting for any man of his size in the world."

Win Tournament.

Besides Otora there are Iwami Yokoyama, Kyko, Kuma and Tanaka, all husky and willing scrappers who are earnestly striving to make themselves proficient in the profession they have adopted.

About a year ago Koriyama took a team of Japanese boxers to Shanghai and cleaned up the Chinese and Filipino knuckle-dusters in an Oriental tournament.

The boxers in Koriyama's stable are clever with their hands, but rather shy, as yet, on the finer points of footwork. Another fault is their tendency to "blow up" when the fighting gets exciting. They are muscular, hard as nails, and by no means lacking in speed. Except for the vaunted prowesses of Otora, however, there are few signs of dynamite in their fists.

Koriyama has an adequately equipped gymnasium at Mikage, where he conducts the Japan Boxing Association. According to Koriyama the raw material from which he hopes to harvest his crop of champions is decidedly promising.

There is one stalwart youth in Koriyama's camp of whom he is especially proud. He is known as "Fighting" Otora.

"That boy has a wallop that would make the heart of Dempsey rejoice." Koriyama declared. "I really think that, when he has leaned a little more about the game, Otora will be able to make things interesting for any man of his size in the world."

Win Tournament

Besides Otora there are Iwami Yokoyama, Kyoko, Kuma and Tanaka, all husky and willing scrappers who are earnestly striving to make themselves more proficient in the profession they have adopted.

About a year ago Koriyama took a team of Japanese boxers to Shanghai and cleaned up the Chinese and Filipino knuckle0dusters in an Oriental tournament.

The boxers in Koriyama's stable are clever with their hands, but rather shy, as yet, on the finer points of footwork. Another fault is their tendency to "blow up" when the fighting gets exciting. They are muscular, hard as nails, and by no means lacking in speed. Except for the vaunted prowess of Otora, however, there are few signs of dynamite in their fists.

April 21ˢᵗ 1932
Santa Cruz Sentinel

Short Stories
By
Russ Newland

By Russ J. Newland

SAN FRANCISCO, April 20 (A)—Young Togo, little Japanese fighter of twenty years ago has been rescued from the Port of Missing Pugilists.

He is a bath house operator in Ardmore, Okla., recovered from blindness that struck him after his last fight in Oakland and evidently enjoying good health in the sunset of life.

Togo was one of the first Japanese to go in for boxing. He also was one of the best of his nationality ever turned out. Yujiro Watanabe, now instructing boxing in Tokyo, appeared on the fistic horizon just after Togo. None of their countrymen has since attained the heights these two Japanese did.

Each fought a champion. Togo exchanged pot-shots with Battling Nelson. Watanabe socked with Willie Ritchie.

Togo went blind after a bout with Roy Moore. An article in this column several weeks ago brought the following information from Ramon Martin of the Daily Ardmorite:

"Your comment about Togo has brought him many letters and I have received several myself from the west coast. Togo is still a fight fan, but that's about all. His fighting days are over, of course, but the old boy still gets a big kick out of taking in fights and he has several proteges that look pretty good, including one little Indian lad about the same build as Togo. He has long since recovered the use of his orbits and has been here in Ardmore for 16 years."

What prompted the writer's article was a paragraph in Sid Zill's column in the Los Angeles Herald-Express inquiring: "Anybody know an ex-pug by the name of Young Togo who gave 'Bat' Nelson quite a fight? He's wanted in Japan on a little matter of inheriting an estate."

Togo's financial status is not known here and the classification of "bath house operator" is not informative toward that end but undoubtedly he will be interested in the matter of "inheriting an estate." So would you, and you, and you.

San Francisco, April 20 Short Stories by Russ Newland

Young Togo, little Japanese fighter of twenty years ago has been rescued from the Port of Missing Pugilists.

He is a bath house operator in Ardmore, Okla., recovered from blindness that struck him after his last fight in Oakland and evidently enjoying good health in the sunset of life.

Togo was one of the first Japanese to go in for boxing. He also was one of the best of his nationality ever turned out. Yujiro Watanabe, now instructing boxing in Tokyo, appeared on the fistic horizon just after Togo. None of their countrymen has since attained the heights these two Japanese did. Each fought a champion. Togo exchanged pot-shots with Battling Nelson. Watanabe socked with Willie Ritchie.

Togo went blind after a bout with Roy Moore. An article in this column several weeks ago brought the following information from Ramon Marton of the Daily Ardmorite:

"Your comment about Togo has brought him many letters and I have received several myself from the west coast. Togo is still a fight fan, but that's about all. His fighting days are over, of course, but the old boy still gets a big kick out of taking in fights and he has several proteges that look pretty good, including one little Indian lad about the same build as Togo. He has long since recovered the use of his orbits and has been here in Armore for 16 years."

What prompted the writer's article was a paragraph in Sid Zill's column in the Los Angeles herald-Express inquiring: "Anybody know an ex-pug by the name of Young Togo who gave 'bat' Nelson quite a fight? He's wanted in Japan on a little matter of inheriting an estate."

Togo's financial status is not known here and the classification of "bath house operator" is not informative toward that end but undoubtedly he will be interested in the matter of "inheriting an estate." So would you , and you , and you.

December 27th 1936
The Oklahoma News Sun

The days that I can recall in the boxing history of Fort Smith were back when Young Togo, a Japanese lightweight, was the boxing star of the city. Togo now lives in Ardmore.

* * *

These days that I can recall in the boxing history of Fort Smith were back when Young Togo, a Japanese lightweight, was the boxing star of the city. Togo now lives in Ardmore.

Watanabe Yujiro's Coaches
Rufus "Rufe" Turner
Charley Turner "The Stockton Cyclone"

Left: Rufus "Rufe" Turner (1877 -1937)
Right: Charley Turner "The Stockton Cyclone" (1862 –1913)

Rufus "Rufe" Turner was an excellent boxer who had a strong punch. He weighed 130-135 pounds. In 1914, he moved to Manila, the Philippines as a boxing instructor and also took occasional bouts winning the Lightweight Championship of the Orient in 1917. His gym may have been called *Boxing School of All Nations.* Overall record: 108 bouts 62 wins 22 losses and 21 draws

His older brother, Charley Turner "The Stockton Cyclone" frequently took on boxers who outweighed him by as much as 20 lbs. Turner's entry in the 1900 census for San Joaquin, California gives his occupation as "Pugilist."

According to Boxing Historian Tony Gee, Charley's longest match was a 49 round draw against a boxer named Billy Mc Rhuson and his second was a loss to Soldier Walker after 23 rounds.

Charley Turner (1862 –1913)
32 Bouts 17 Wins (16 KO) 8 Loss 7 Draw
Source: Boxrec

July 20ᵗʰ 1884
The San Francisco Examiner

> **Glove Fight at Stockton.**
> STOCKTON, July 19.—The glove fight at
> the National Hall this evening between
> Frank Frayne of San Francisco, and
> Charley Turner, a Stockton amateur, was
> won in eight rounds by Turner. It was
> the best fight ever witnessed here.

Glove Fight at Stockton

Stockton, July 19. – The glove fight at the National Hall this evening between Frank Frayne of San Francisco, and Charley Turner, a Stockton amateur, was won in eight rounds by Turner. It was the best fight ever witnessed here.

September 22ⁿᵈ 1884
The San Francisco Examiner

> J. C. Seymour, Harry Maynard's man-
> ager, says he has arranged a match in
> Stockton for the 27th instant between Jim
> Hall and Charley Turner for $100 a side.
> The fight will be with hard gloves,
> Queensberry rules, to a finish.

J.C. Seymour, Harry Maynard's manager, says he has arranged a match in Stockton for the 27the instant between Jim Hall and Charley Turner for $100 a side. The fight will be with hard gloves, Queensberry rules[32], to a finish.

---

[32] A code of generally accepted rules for boxing drafted in London in 1865. It includes:
1.   To be a fair stand-up boxing match in a 24-foot ring,
2.   No wrestling allowed.
3.   The rounds to be of 3 minutes' duration, and 1 minute's time between rounds.
In addition to the 10 count system for downs.

November 23rd 1892 The Salt Lake Herald

TURNER MAY COME.

Salt Lakers Anxious to See the Stockton Cyclone.

It will not be a Fight to a Finish, but a Six-Round Contest Between Him and Jim Williams.

There are a great many people in this city who would like to see Charley Turner, the Stockton cyclone, who so cleverly got in his licks on Jim Williams in the early part of the battle, and who so pluckily stood up as long as his legs would hold him.

Turner was the only man Jim ever met who could hit him four times and safely get away before he knew what had struck him.

This may be but a forcible illustration that motion is quicker than sight, and the black man from the Pacific as a slight-of-hand performer is certainly a success.

A FIGHT TO A FINISH between the two men is not to be thought of for two reasons. In the first place Turner, after trying to stand up against the Utah champion for eleven rounds, is satisfied with the results and does not care at this early day to repeat the dose that he was compelled to take. In the second place it is questionable whether Mayor Baskin would consent to afford the admirers of pugilism such a treat, even though the men were to agree to a finish fight, but it is believed that his honor will allow the boys the privilege of seeing the Utah boy meet the man whom he vanquished in a friendly glove contest of six rounds, in which no serious damage will be done.

Turner May Come. Salt Lakers Anxious to See the Stockton Cyclone. It will not be a Fight to a Finish, but a Six-round Contest Between Him and Jim Williams

There are a great many people in this city who would like to see Charley Turner, the Stockton cyclone, who so cleverly got in his licks on Jim Williams in the early part of the battle, and who so pluckily stood up as long as his legs would hold him.

Turner was the only man Jim ever met who could hit him four times and safely get away before he knew what had struck him.

This may be but a forcible illustration that motion is quicker than sight, and the black man from the Pacific as a slight-of-hand performer is certainly a success.

A Fight to a finish between the two men is not to be thought of for two reasons. In the first place Turner, after trying to stand up against the Utah champion for eleven rounds, is satisfied with the results and does not care at this early day to repeat the dose that he was compelled to take. In the second place it is questionable whether Mayor Baskin would consent to afford the admirers of pugilism such a treat, even though the men were to agree to a finish fight, but it is believed that his honor will allow the boys the privilege of seeing the Utah boy meet the man whom he vanquished in a friendly glove contest of six rounds, in which no serious damage will be done.

February 10th 1913
Stockton Daily Evening Record

CHARLEY TURNER IN ACTION AGAIN

His Face Is a Study When There Is a Black Man in the Ring

It was during the fourth round of the fight between Kid Reese, the clever colored boxer, and a husky young white pugilist last Wednesday night at the Hub City Athletic Club that Charley Turner, the veteran colored boxer, fought a fast and furious round with himself forty or fifty feet away from the padded ring.

Turner was a spectator. He stood against the south wall. He favored Reese, the colored boy. He wanted Reese to win. He had watched the contest through three hotly contested rounds, and evidently began to think the white man was a good one. Turner was hoarse—he could not shout words of encouragement loud enough to be heard by Reese—his voice would not carry to the ring. But from his facial expressions and continuous talk, one seated near him knew exactly how the round was being fought without once glancing toward the contestants. The gong sounded for the wind-up round, and both fighters advanced quickly from their corners. Here's how Turner, from his position near the south wall, coached Kid Reese, who, however, never heard a word that was uttered.

Steady now, Reese! Steady now. Don't leave an openin: don't leave an openin'! Lear yer left! Quick now! That's it—that's it! Good boy, Reese. Good boy! Plant him again, Reese. Look out, Reese! Look out for that right—keep yer eye open, Reese; keep yer eye open! Wow! But that didn't hurt, Reese! That didn't hurt much—on'y a light tap! Now, go it, Reese! Go it! He can't hurt ye—good boy, Reese! Knock his block off! Knock his block off, Reese! Follow him up, Reese! Follow him up! He's got no show with you, Reese—no show at all. Huh! Oh, Reese, look out for that left. Now, upper cut him! Drive in yer left, Reese—that's it, work yer right, too! Huh! Them punches on the nose, don't hurt, Reese—he can't reach ye hard enough to hurt. That's it! That's it, Reese—now ye got him! Now ye got him! Send yer left home hard, Reese! Drive in yer right, Reese! Huh, say, what's that? (as the gong sounded and the referee raised the white man's arm, declaring him the winner)—what's that? Lost the decision, Reese! Gawd! Ye oughter knocked his block off.

And Charley Turner subsided. He had fought the fight for Reese with all the old time prowess he could summon. His face was a study for the three minutes of fast fighting. When Reese was hit hard Charley would wince. When Reese was the aggressor Charley would endeavor to encourage him. It was more interesting to watch Turner, who at one time was one of the best boxers Stockton claimed, than to have watched the mill inside the ropes.

Charley Turner in Action Again
His Face is a Study When There Is a Black Man in The Ring

It was during the fourth round of the fight between Kid Reese, the clever colored boxer, and a husky young white pugilist last Wednesday night at the Hub City Athletic Club that Charley Turner, the veteran colored boxer, fought a fast and furious round with himself forty of fifty feet away from the padded ring.

Turner was a spectator. He stood against the south wall. He favored Reese, the colored boy. He wanted Reese to win. He had watched the contest through three hotly contested rounds, and evidently began to think the white man was a good one. Turner was hoarse - he could not shout words of encouragement loud enough to be heard by Reese – his voice would not carry to the ring. But from his facial expressions and continuous talk, one seated hear him knew exactly how the round was being fought without once glancing toward the contestants. The gong sounded for the wind-up round, and both fighters advanced quickly from their corners here's how Turner, from his position near the south wall, coached Kid Reese, who, however, never heard a word that was uttered.

Steady now, Reese! Steady now. Don't leave an openin': don't leave an openin'! Lear yer left! Quick now! That's it – that's it! Good boy, Reese. Good boy! Plant him again, Reese. Look out, Reese! Look out for that right – keep yer eye open, Reese: keep yer eye open! Wow! But that didn't hurt, Reese! That didn't hurt much – on'y a light tap! Now go it, Reese! Go it! He can't hurt ye – good boy Reese! Knock is block off! Knock his block off, Reese! Follow him up, Reese! Follow him up! He's got no show with you, Reese – no show at all. Huh! Oh, Reese, look out for that left. Now, upper cut him! Drive in yer left, Reese – that's it, work yer right, too! Huh! Them punches on the nose, don't hurt, Reese – he can't reach ye hard enough to hurt. That's it! That's it, Reese – now ye got him" Now ye got him! Send yer left home hard, Reese! Drive in yer right, Reese! Huh, say, what's that?(as the gong sounded and the referee raised the white man's arm, declaring him the inner) – what's that? Lost the decision, Reese! Gawd! Ye outer knocked his block off.

And Charley Turner subsided. He had fought the fight for Reese with all the old time prowess he could summon. His face was a study for the three minutes of fast fighting. When Reese was hit hard Charley would wince. When Reese was the aggressor Charley would endeavor to encourage him. It was more interesting to watch Turner, who at one time was one of the best boxers Stockton claimed, than to have watched the mill inside the ropes.

August 13th 1913
The Los Angeles Times

CHARLEY TURNER DIES.

STOCKTON, Aug. 12.—[By A. P. Night Wire.] Charley Turner, the "Stockton Cyclone" of bygone days, and one of the best ring generals that ever donned a glove, died today at the home of his aged mother, where he had been ill for several weeks. "Rufe" Turner, also a boxer, was at the bedside when Charley "took the count." The veteran fighter was aged 51 years, and had not been active in pugilistic events during the past twenty years.

Charley Turner Dies

Stockton, Aug. 12 – Charley Turner, the "Stockton Cyclone" of bygone days, and one of the best ring generals that ever donned a glove, died today at the home of his aged mother, where he had been ill for several weeks. "Rufe" Turner, also a boxer, was at the bedside when Charley "took the count." The veteran fighter was aged 51 years, and had not been active in pugilistic events during the past 20 years.

Rutherford "Rufe" Turner (1877 ~ 1937)
108 Bouts 62 Wins (42 by KO) 22 Losses 21 Draw
Source: Boxrec

Rufe Turner of California in 1905

May 25th 1896
The Evening Mail (Stockton California)

GENTLEMEN'S NIGHT,

At the Stockton Athletic Association's
Clubhouse.

The coming gentlemen's night at the
Stockton Athletic Asociation's clubhouse will be one of the best things
of its kind that has yet been given
here. George Green, better known as
"Young Corbett" who recently secured the decision over Owen Zeigler in
an eight round contest in San Francisco, will be on hand and will spar
with Willis Armstrong, the boxing instructor of the club. There will be two
eight-round contest for points. One of
these has already been arranged and
will be between Rufe Turner, a brother
of Charley Turner, Stockton's celebrated colored pugilist, and Ben Maxwell.
The other match has not yet been
settled upon but will probably be between two clever boxers from San
Francisco, who will show what skill
and science with the gloves can do.
Instructor Armstrong, who is arranging the entertainment, will also secure
the services of Lewis Meyers, the club
swinger of the Olympic Club, for the
occasion. George Green will act as
referee in the eight-round contest. The
entertainment is to be an invitation affair.

Gentlemen's Night
At the Stockton Athletic Association's Clubhouse

The coming gentlemen's night at the Stockton Athletic Association's clubhouse will be one of the best things of its kind that has yet been given here. George Green, better known as "Young Corbett" who recently secured the decision over Owen Zeigler in an eight round contest in San Francisco, will be on hand and will spar with Willis Armstrong, the boxing instructor of the club. There will be two eight-round contest for points. One of these has already been arranged and will be between Rufe Turner, a brother of Charley Turner, Stockton's celebrated colored pugilist, and Ben Maxwell. The other match has not yet been settled upon but will probably be between two clever boxers from San Francisco, who will show what skill and science with the gloves can do. Instructor Armstrong, who is arranging the entertainment, will also secure the services of Lewis Meyers, the club swinger of the Olympic Club, for the occasion. George Green will act as the referee in the eight-round contest. The entertainment is to be an invitation affair.

January 6ᵗʰ 1898 Oakland Tribune

RALSTON NO MATCH FOR RUFE TURNER.

The Lockeford Boy Goes Down Before the Stockton Lad

By Associated Press to The Tri...

STOCKTON, Cal., Jan. 6.—Rufe Turner of Stockton, a brother of Charlie Turner, and Bert Ralston, the son of a well-known farmer of Lockeford, were matched last night for a ten-round contest before the Lockeford Athletic Club of that town.

The men were pretty fairly matched as to weight, but the Lockeford lad was no match for the colored boy of this city.

The fight was declared off after the fourth round, Ralston's seconds throwing up the sponge. Both men sparred continuously for a few moments, when Turner landed squarely, sending the young rancher to the floor. Turner then had things all his own way, getting in blow after blow.

During the four rounds, Ralston was knocked down ten times, but he showed remarkable grit and each time was up and facing his opponent, before he could be counted out. When his seconds threw up the sponge he protested, declaring that he could not be knocked out.

Very little money was exchanged on the fight, for which there was plenty of Turner money. The backers of the Lockeford boy would not take it up.

Ralston No Match for Rufe Turner
The Lockeford Boy Goes Down Before the Stockton Lad

Stockton, Cal. Jan. 6. – Rufe Turner of Stockton, a brother of Charlie Turner, and Bert Ralston, the son of a well-known farmer of Lockeford, were matched last night for a ten-round contest before the Lockeford Athletic Club of that town.

The men were pretty fairly matched, as to weight, but the Lockeford lad was no match for the colored boy of this city.

The fight was declared off after the fourth round, Ralston's seconds throwing up the sponge. Both men sparred continuously for a few moments, when Turner landed squarely, sending the young rancher to the floor. Turner then had things all his own way, getting in blow after blow.

During the four rounds, Ralston was knocked down ten times, but he showed remarkable grit and each time was up and facing his opponent, before he could be counted out. When his seconds threw up the sponge he protested, declaring that he could not be knocked out.

Very little money was exchanged on the fight, for which there was plenty of Turner money. The backers of the Lockeford boy would not take it up.

September 4th 1901 Oakland Tribune

For the regular monthly exhibition,
which takes place on the evening of
September 19th the ' club has secured
talent which is above the average. For
the main event Perry Queenan,   the
well-known Chicago lad, who recently
fought a fast twenty round draw with
Rufe Turner, has been secured for a
fifteen-round bout with Henry Lewis,
the well-known San Francisco colored
lightweight.   Jack Capeliss will   be

For the regular monthly exhibition, which takes place on the evening of September 19th the club has secured talent which is above the average. For the main event Perry Queenan, the well-known Chicago lad, who recently fought a fast twenty round draw with Rufe Turner, has been secured for a fifteen-round bout with Henry Lewis, the well-known San Francisco colored lightweight.

March 20th 1902 Oakland Tribune

Beside the main event, there will be
a contest between Rufe Turner and
Jack O'Brien, which on any other occasion would be regarded as a main
event. This will be the second meeting
between these men, O'Brien having
won the first engagement at Stockton.

Besides the main event, there will be a contest between Rufe Turner and Jack O'Brien, which on any other occasion would be regarded as a main event. This will be the second meeting between these men. O'brien having won the first engagement at Stockton.

July 4th 1902
Oakland Tribune

▸LEWIS LASTS TWO ROUNDS AT STOCKTON

RUFE TURNER BRINGS HIM DOWN WITH A PUNCH ON THE CHIN.

STOCKTON, July 4.—Rufe Turner, the Stockton lightweight boxer, sent Willie Lewis of New York to dreamland in the second round of a twenty-round fight last night with a right counter. Lewis made a fine showing and used both hands to good advantage, but it was simply a case of colliding with Turner's sledge hammer punch, which always put out the colored boy's opponent.

Turner rushed and was stopped with a left jab. He sent in a right cross to the point of the chin and Lewis was counted out long before he recovered consciousness. He was groggy an hour after the fight. The betting was 10 to 4, with Turner the favorite. Now Turner wants a chance at Gans at the lightweight limit.

Lewis Lasts Two Rounds At Stockton
Rufe Turner Brings Him Down With a Punch On The Chin

Stockton, July 4. – Rufe Turner, the Stockton lightweight boxer, sent Willie Lewis of New York to dreamland in the second round of a twenty-round fight last night with a right counter. Lewis made a fine showing and used both hands to good advantage, but it was simply a case of colliding with Turner's sledge hammer punch, which always put out the colored boy's opponent.

Turner rushed and was stopped with a left jab. He sent in a right cross to the point of the chin and Lewis was counted out long before he recovered consciousness. He was groggy an hour after the fight. The betting was 10 to 4, with Turner the favorite. Now Turner wants a chance at Gans at the lightweight limit.

July 15th 1902
Oakland Tribune

GANS-TURNER FIGHT WILL DRAW A CROWD

SPECIAL TRAIN WILL BE RUN FROM STOCKTON TO OAKLAND.

The admirers of Rufe Turner in the vicinity of Stockton have chartered a special train to run down the night of the fight with Gans at the Acme Club. Turner is looked upon as invincible in Stockton. His wonderful showing in the ring of late has set his stock away up. The Acme Club has received orders for reserved seats to be set aside for the Turner contingent to the amount of 200.

The Acme Club will make special arrangements to handle this contest owing to the immense crowd that is expected. Turner has a large following which will stake their last dollar on his chances with Gans. Among the wise bettors it is conceded that Turner has a splendid chance in this fight at the weight signed—135 pounds, ring side.

JOE GANS

RUFE TURNER.

Gans (left) Turner (right) Fight Will Draw A Crowd
Special Train Will Be Run From Stockton To Oakland

The admirers of Rufe Turner in the vicinity of Stockton have chartered a special train to run down the night of the fight with Gans at the Acme Club. Turner is looked upon as invincible in Stockton. His wonderful showing in the ring of late has set his stock away up. The Acme Club has received orders for reserved seats to be set aside for the Turner contingent to the amount of 200.

The Acme Club will make special arrangements to handle this contest owing to the immense crowd that is expected. Turner has a large following which will stake their last dollar on his chances with Gans. Among the wise betters it is conceded that Turner has a splendid chance in this fight at the weigh singed – 135 pounds, ring side.[33]

---

[33] Gans won by knockout.

October 18ᵗʰ 1911
Oakland Tribune

GOLDEN GATE CLUB HAS GOOD CARD FOR FRIDAY NIGHT

The Golden Gate Club offers an attractive card for Friday night at Dreamland pavilion. In the windup Charlie Reilly, the clever local lightweight who has been doing so much training at Al White's camp, will clash with "Kid" Dalton, the tough little scrapper from Los Angeles. Dalton is a two-handed fighter with a punch and as he is always boring in, he should make a good opponent for a scientific lad such as Reilly. This will be the main event of an eight-bout program.

Charlie Miller and Ed Dunkhorst, heavyweights, will tangle in the joke scrap of the night. These two burlies make the scales quiver around the 600-pound mark and there should be lots of fun dispensed when they begin to move about on the platform.

The middleweight go between Kid George and Rufe Williams should be a hummer. These middleweights are well matched and as George has been doing some sensational milling lately he figures to turn the tables on the colored pugilist.

The rest of the card is as follows: Rufe Turner vs. Billy Walters, Dummy Thomas vs. Kid Harvey, Lee Johnson vs. Billy Chappelle; Yujiro Watanabe vs. Kid Schiff and another four-round preliminary.

Golden Gate Club Has Good Card For Friday Night

The Golden Gate Club offers an attractive card for Friday night at Dreamland pavilion. In the windup Charlie Reilly, the clever local lightweight who has been doing so much training at Al White's camp, will clash with "Kid" Dalton, the tough little scrapper from Los Angeles. Dalton is a two-handed fighter with a punch and as he is always boring in, he should make a good opponent for a scientific lad such as Reilly. This will be the main event of an eight-bout program.

Charlie Miller and Ed Dunkhorst, heavyweights, will tangle in the joke scrap of the night. These two burlies make the scales quiver around the 600-pound mark and there should be lots of fun dispensed when they begin to move about on the platform.

The middleweight go between Kid George and Rufe Williams should be a hummer. These middleweights are well matched and as George has been doing some sensational milling lately he figures to turn the tables on the colored pugilist.

The rest of the card is as follows.: Rufe Turner vs. Billy Walters, Dummy Thomas vs Kid Harvey, Lee Johnson vs. Billy Chappelle: Yujiro Watanabe vs. Kid Schiff and another four-round preliminary.

June 8th 1921 Oakland Tribune

RUFE TURNER, OLD TIMER, STILL IN THE RING

STOCKTON, June 8.—Rufe Turner, 20 years ago aspirant for lightweight honors, and one of the best men of his weight in the country at that time, is still fighting—and successfully. He writes to an old Stockton friend from the Island of Cebu that he is instructor of a new athletic club there, fighting occasionally and prospering. Rufe tells of his wealth in lands and houses and states he is happily married. Recently he knocked out a big fellow in three rounds and, allowed another to stay for a draw, hoping for another fight, but the bird ran out on him. Turner, a native of Stockton, is a brother of Charley Turner, once a noted lightweight himself. Rufe had an awful wallop, but didn't like to train. However, he lived a clean life and now it is telling, for despite his 40-odd years he is still young in mind and body and able to go the route.

Rufe Turner, Old Timer, Still in the Ring

Stockton, June 8 – Rufe Turner, 20 years ago aspirant for lightweight honors, and one of the best men of his weight in the country at the time, is still fighting – and successfully. He writes to an old Stockton friend from the Island of Cebu that he is instructor of a new athletic club there, fighting occasionally and prospering. Rufe tells of his wealth in lands and houses and states he is happily married. Recently he knocked out a big fellow in three rounds and, allowed another to stay for a draw, hoping for another fight, but the bird ran out on him. Turner, a native of Stockton, is a brother of Charley turner, once a noted lightweight himself. Rufe had an awful wallop, but didn't like to train. However, he lived a clean life and now it is telling, for despite his 40 – odd years he is still young in mind and body and able to go the route.[34]

---

[34] According to this excerpt from *Escape from New York: The New Negro Renaissance beyond Harlem* by Davarian L. Baldwin Rufe Turner went to the Philippines in 1914:
"The boxing scene in Manila also expanded, opening up new opportunities for black pugilists looking to dodge the Jim Crow color line in the U.S. boxing scene. African American lightweight Rufus Turner arrived in the capital in July 1914. A professional boxer since 1893, Turner was a veteran hoping for a chance to extend the life of his pugilistic career. He worked as a trainer, a referee, and a prizefighter. Over the course of seven years he fought against numerous American, Australian and Filipino opponents."

July 3rd 1927 Stockton Independent

"Rufe" Turner, Once Famed Stockton Colored Battler, In Manila Insane Asylum

Rufe Turner, colored boy, formerly of Stockton, on whom Stocktonians won and lost thousands of dollars while his somewhat sensational rise in the prize ring was in progress twenty-five and thirty years ago, is in an insane asylum at Manila, Philippine islands, according to word received here. Turner believes that his brother, "Budge" Turner, who still lives here, is in Manila and is endeavoring to kill him in order to obtain property which Rufe says he owns in this city.

The following is a copy of a letter addressed "To His Honor the Mayor of Stockton, Cal." by H. E. Brinson, plumbing contractor of Manila:

"Sir: I have the honor to request of you information of one Virgil Turner reported to be living in Stockton. Here living in Manila is one by name Rutherford B. Rogers, an old prize fighter who went under the name of Rufe Turner.

"The said Rufe Turner has recently been sent to the insane asylum. But before being sent to the asylum he lived with me about two months. He claims to have a half-brother by the name of Virgil Turner. If your honor would kindly notify this half-brother to get in touch with me, I could give him all necessary information regarding the said Rufe Turner.

"I am almost certain that a letter to the Director of Health here with full assurance that he would be well looked after by his relatives in Stockton would obtain his transfer.

"Rufe is perfectly harmless, he only imagines his brother is trying to kill him in order to obtain some property he claims to own in Stockton. He actually believes his brother is here in Manila.

"Dr. Domingo, a specialist on insanity advised me to get in touch with his brother and if possible have him send for Rufe. The doctor seems to think that if Rufe could meet his brother that he could be cured of his illusion.

"Thanking your honor in advance for the trouble I am asking of you, I am,

"Yours respectfully,
(Signed) "H. E. BRINSON."

The Mayor's office turned the letter over to "Budge" Turner, who had a friend make reply.

"Budge" has neither the desire to go to Manila nor to have Rufe returned here, both for financial reasons and otherwise.

"Rufe" Turner and his other brother, "Charlie" Turner were familiar figures some twenty-five or thirty years ago. Both were prominent in the roped arena and fought their way up to about the top rung of the ladder in the lightweight class, reaching the position of near-great but not quite able to grasp the coveted laurels. Charlie and Rufe fought most of the best men in their class.

"Charlie" was rated as one of the most finished boxers in the ring during his time. Many of Stockton's business and professional men of 30 and 35 years ago used to take boxing lessons from him. Rufe followed in Charlie's footsteps and either knocked out or won decisions over the big men in his class. Success, with the accompanying conviviality, the common thing at that time among pugilists, played havoc with their condition and it was the same old tale of going down hill, fighting third-raters and finally dropping out of the game. Charlie died some years ago and no one seemed to know to where Rufe disappeared. According to one who knew him in his palmy days he is about 49 years of age now. It is said that he was married in Manila to a Filipino.

"Budge" Turner may still be seen about the streets of Stockton. He does odd jobs of janitor work, but was well known in sporting circles when "Charlie" and "Rufe" were in their prime.

Both the fighters were ebony black in color and the sight of their glistening skins in the roped square was the signal of wild enthusiasm on the part of the fight fans and their admirers and backers, who numbered judges, lawyers and other professional men and many of the big business men of the city. To thousands of them who are here today this story will recall the "days of real sport" and they will be sorry to hear of the present plight of one who was considered a physical wonder in his prime. Rufe fought local battles in the gym at the corner of Hunter and Weber, at the old Agricultural pavilion, the Avon theater and the auditorium in the old Masonic Temple.

"Rufe" Turner, Once Famed Stockton Colored Battler, In Manila Insane Asylum

Rufe Turner, colored boy, formerly of Stockton, on whom Stocktonians won and lost thousands of dollars while his somewhat sensational rise in the prize ring was in progress twenty-five and thirty years ago, is in an insane asylum at Manila, Philippine Islands, according to word received here. Turner believes that his brother, "Budge" Turner, who still lives here, is in Manila and is endeavoring to kill him in order to obtain property which Rufe says he owns in this city.

The following is a copy of a letter addressed "To His Honor the Mayor of Stockton, Cal." By H.E. Brinson, plumbing contractor of Manila:

Sir: I have the honor to request of you information of one Virgil Turner reported to be living in Stockton. Here living in Manila is one by name Rutherford B. Rogers, an old prize fighter who went under the name of Rufe Turner.

The said Rufe Turner has recently been sent to the insane asylum. But before being sent to the asylum he lived with me about two months. He claims to have a half-brother by the name of Virgil Turner. If your honor would kindly notify this half-brother to get in touch with me, I could give him all necessary information regarding the said Rufe Turner.

I am almost certain that a letter to the Director of Health here with full assurance that he would be well looked after by his relatives in Stockton would obtain his transfer.

Rufe is perfectly harmless, he only imagines his brother is trying to kill him in order to obtain some property he claims to own in Stockton. He actually believes his brother is here in Manila.

Dr. Domingo, a specialist on insanity advised me to get in touch with his brother and if possible have him send for Rufe. The doctor seems to think that if Rufe could meet his brother that he could be cured of his illusion.

Thanking your honor in advance for the trouble I am asking of you, I am.

Yours respectfully, (signed) "H.E. Brinson."

The Mayor's office turned the letter over to "Budge" Turner who had a friend make reply. "Budge" has neither the desire to go to Manila nor to have Rufe retuned here, both for financial reasons and otherwise.

"Rufe" Turner and his other brother, "Charlie" Turner were familiar figures some twenty-five or thirty years ago. Both were prominent in the roped arena and fought their way up to about the top rung of the ladder in the lightweight class, reaching the position of near-great but not quite able to grasp the coveted laurels. Charlie and Rufe fought most of the best men in their class.

"Charlie" was rated as one of the most finished boxers in the ring during his time. Many of Stockton's businesses and professional men of 30 and 35 years ago used to take boxing lessons from him. Rufe followed in Charlie's footsteps and either knocked out or won decisions over the big men in his class. Success, with the accompanying conviviality, the common thing at that time among pugilists, played havoc with their condition and it was the same old tale of going downhill, fighting third-raters, and finally dropping out of the game. Charlie died some years ago and no one seemed to know where Rufe disappeared. According to one who knew him in his palmy days he is about 49 years of age now. It is said that he was married in Manila to a Filipino.

"Budge" Turner may still be seen about the streets of Stockton. He does odd jobs of janitor work, but was well known in sporting circles when "Charlie" and "Rufe" were in their prime.

Both of the fighters were ebony black in color and the sight of their glistening skins in the roped square was the signal of wild enthusiasm on the part of the fight fans and their admirers and backers, who numbered judges, lawyers and other professional men and many of the big businessmen of the city. To thousands of them who are here today this story will recall the "days of real sport" and they will be sorry to hear of the present plight of one who was considered a physical wonder in his prime. Rufe fought local battles in the gym at the corner of Hunter and Weber, at the old Agricultural pavilion, the Avon theater, and the auditorium in the old Masonic temple.

July 10th 1937
The Press Democrat (Santa Rosa, California)

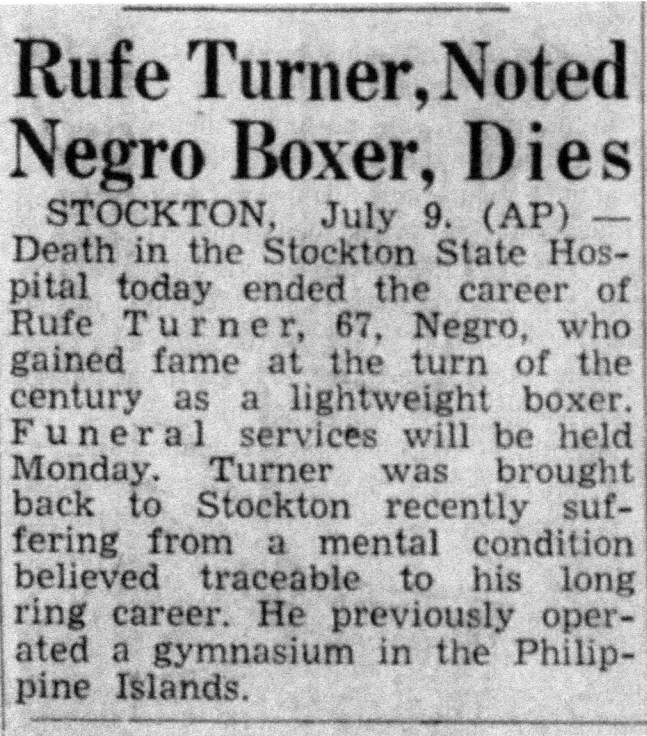

Rufe Turner, Noted Negro Boxer, Dies

STOCKTON, July 9. (AP) — Death in the Stockton State Hospital today ended the career of Rufe Turner, 67, Negro, who gained fame at the turn of the century as a lightweight boxer. Funeral services will be held Monday. Turner was brought back to Stockton recently suffering from a mental condition believed traceable to his long ring career. He previously operated a gymnasium in the Philippine Islands.

Rufe Turner, Noted Negro Boxer, Dies

Stockton, July 9. – Death in the Stockton State Hospital today ended the career of Rufe Turner, 67, Negro, who gained fame at the turn of the century as a lightweight boxer. Funeral services will be held Monday. Turner was brought back to Stockton recently suffering from a mental condition believed traceable to his long ring career. He previously operated a gymnasium in the Philippine Islands.

www.ingramcontent.com/pod-product-compliance
Lightning Source LLC
Chambersburg PA
CBHW050123280326
41933CB00010B/1229